CUSTOMER SERVICE

in the Motor Trade

by

BILL NAYLOR FIMI

Published by:
The Institute of the Motor Industry
Fanshaws
Brickendon
Hertford
SG13 8PQ

First published 1995
Second edition 1997
© 1997 The Institute of the Motor Industry

ISBN 1 871880 39 4

Publications Manager: Peter Creasey FIMI
Education Manager: Alan Mackrill MBA BEd(Hons) LAE FIMI AssIPD
Series Editor: Harry Darton BSc(Econ)

Designed by: Julian Bennett, Hertford

Originating, printing and binding in Great Britain by:
Black Bear Press Ltd
Kings Hedges Road
Cambridge
CB4 2PQ

THE UNDERPINNING KNOWLEDGE SERIES

Books in the Underpinning Knowledge series, published by The Institute of the Motor Industry, are:

CUSTOMER SERVICE in the Motor Trade
by Bill Naylor FIMI   ISBN 1 871880 39 4

VEHICLE PARTS Administration and Organization
by Tom Colley LAE MIMI   ISBN 1 871880 14 9

VEHICLE MECHANICAL AND ELECTRONIC SYSTEMS
by Andrew Livesey BEd(Hons),IEng,LAE,FIMI

                                             ISBN 1 871880 19 X

VEHICLE FINISHING
by Charles Long MIMI   ISBN 1 871880 29 7

MANAGEMENT in the Motor Trade
by Jill Blacklin CertEd,DMS,MBA   ISBN 1 871880 34 3

VEHICLE BODY REPAIR
by Alan Rennie MIMI LAE LCG   ISBN 1 871880 24 6

Enquiries regarding this series and orders for the books should be addressed to:

Publications Manager
The Institute of the Motor Industry
Fanshaws
Brickendon
Hertford
SG13 8PQ
Tel: 01992 511521
Fax: 01992 511548

PUBLISHER'S INTRODUCTION

This book, while giving a general outline of the subject, has been designed primarily to help in the knowledge and understanding required for National Vocational Qualifications (NVQs) in Customer Service.

NVQs are based on national standards required for employment and as such cover all sectors and levels of employment. The assessment of these qualifications is based on a person's ability to show his or her competence against the standards which have been defined. There are no set courses of study or training and the assessment is carried out when the candidate is ready, not when the assessor decrees. There is no pass or failure; the person concerned is either competent or not-yet-competent.

'Competence' means being able to perform the job to the standards expected by employers in the industry. The NVQ is broken down into **Units of Competence**, each of which covers a reasonably self-contained aspect of the occupation. The Units are further sub-divided into **Elements of Competence** and then into **Performance Criteria**. It is against the Performance Criteria with the Range Statements and Knowledge that the candidate is assessed.

While competence is measured in the actual DOING of the task, there is obviously a need for underlying knowledge which the candidate must have in order to be able actually to carry out the practical work involved. This, known in NVQ terms as The Underpinning Knowledge, is the subject matter of this book.

To relate the material here to the part of the NVQ being covered, there are indicators used. The **Unit** is used as the chapter heading and sub-headings indicate the **Elements**. Further sub-division breaks the Elements up into the required **Performance Criteria**, formal setting out of which appears in the text. To assist those who select from the book at the time of familiarising themselves with a *specific* Performance Criteria, the Underpinning Knowledge is detailed in that section, with some information perhaps repeated from other Performance Criteria, or a cross-reference is given to the related section or sections.

The Institute of the Motor Industry, publisher of this series of books, is the major awarding body for NVQs in the motor industry. We wish all our readers following the NVQ trail great success in their careers and hope that this information will bolster their abilities to perform their jobs to the best possible levels of competence and to their greatest satisfaction.

It is, however, our hope that readers will not see the NVQ as the end of the qualification trail, but rather the beginning. On successful completion of your NVQ programme, we look forward to welcoming you into membership of the Institute of the Motor Industry. Our letters after your name will identify you to the world in general as a dedicated professional, will serve as witness to your total competence and your full commitment to your industry and your career.

ROY WARD FIMI
Director General
The Institute of the Motor Industry

Preface

Having just spent nearly a year and over 300 hours studying and researching for my own NVQ level 5 in management within the motor industry, I just cannot explain how elated I was when in February 1995 I presented my completed portfolio and undertook my final oral assessment to show that I had the underpinning knowledge and was awarded my certificate.

After 36 years in the motor industry, starting as a motor mechanic through to being managing director of a group of companies, I felt it would be very easy to show that I had the 'can do' ability and the underpinning knowledge and understanding to obtain the highest level in National Vocational Qualifications.

How wrong could I be! To start with I needed to have determination to set aside my valuable leisure time, to research the actions I had taken over the years in doing my job, and to ensure that I could prove that I achieved the performance criteria in all the Units and various Elements of my NVQ. Often I became despondent and disheartened when I just could not get my head round certain elements and if it was not for my assessor appointed by the Institute of the Motor Industry I would probably have fallen by the wayside.

When I was asked to write this text book for Customer Service, covering the knowledge and understanding of this very important NVQ, I jumped at the opportunity of sharing my experiences of best practice in serving the motoring public.

I will have achieved something even if it just enables candidates to understand quickly the importance of the high performance criteria required to achieve Levels 2 and 3 in Customer Service; if it improves the relationships between themselves and their customers, who pay their wages; plus raises their own esteem within their company.

The contents of this textbook are by no means definitive, as many companies, manufacturers, and importers have their own ideas. However, I will share with you what I consider to be best practice, which will enable you to prove your 'can do' ability and provide you with understanding and knowledge in relation to this very important National Vocational Qualification, Customer Service.

Bill Naylor FIMI

Contents

INTRODUCTION TO CUSTOMER SERVICE
LEVEL 2 UNITS

Key Purpose: **DELIVER CONTINUOUS IMPROVEMENT IN SERVICE TO ACHIEVE CUSTOMER SATISFACTION**

Customer Service Level 2 has five main units and within those units are 15 elements, which have 73 performance criteria to be met.

These NVQ UNITS are ideal for service receptionists, sales admin, technicians, parts, front- and back-counter staff - in fact any customer-facing team member - and can be obtained individually.

When you get your portfolio do not panic, your assessor will take you through it step-by-step. Just read it through several times, looking at the performance criteria required for each element.

In the following pages I will try to outline some of the areas in which you may be involved in doing your job, which, if carried out to a high standard, will enable you to have the understanding and knowledge, or at least stimulate your thinking in other directions as to what affects Customer Service.

LEVEL 2 - UNIT 1

OPERATE SERVICE DELIVERY SYSTEMS FOR CUSTOMERS

This unit is made up of four elements; the first being:

1.1 Deliver products or services to Customers

1.1.1 Products or services of the organisation are promptly supplied when asked for

In the case of service or parts, customers coming in are not there because they want to be and often are apprehensive. Their understanding of the differences between an A service or a B service can be limited; in addition, their knowledge of motor industry jargon can make them uneasy, especially if they are ladies. Specialist language - such as back order, VOR, vin number - should be avoided.

Menu Price boards, and up-to-date accessory lists should be used. In-depth explanation should be given regarding what is covered in a service, so that the customer is not disappointed when they come to collect their car only to find that the engine-tune they wanted and expected was not covered by the service.

1.1.2 Other products and services are suggested to meet customers' needs

It is often very natural, especially when we are busy, just to give the customer what they ask for. The customer who is at the parts front counter, for example, has their model number and chassis number and they ask for a water pump. We give it to them, take their money and are very polite. You have done everything right... or have you? When the customer gets home and takes off the old pump, they find that they also needed a gasket and rubber seal, so they have to come back. They just might think you were not all that professional.

So remember to put yourself in your customer's shoes. Are there any additional products or services that you could suggest to meet the customer's needs?

1.1.3 Customer product or service needs are explored through sensitive questioning

Remember, the customer in front of you feels as if they are going into hospital. Will you find anything seriously wrong, will you have the cure, will they be out tonight. Or will we say: try this and if it's not any better in a week come back and see me. How often have we heard that at the doctors?

Sensitive questioning and defining of what the customer wants is so important. Don't let's have: 'Next have you got your voucher book? No? You will have to go get it then. Did you not see the sign to bring your book in with you?' Yes, this attitude still goes on today, but not with professionals.

Customers have statutory rights and therefore it is important that, when defining customers' needs, we are careful of what we say. Without knowing it, we could commit our company to a verbal contract, which could have expensive consequences if we are unable to fulfil their needs.

For example, if we told the customer their car would have a full bumper-to-bumper check during the service, and later the exhaust fell off, we could be held responsible because of the way we described the service we were offering in the first place.

Customers do like to feel that, when they hand over their pride and joy, you will care for it just as they do.

1.1.4 Own knowledge of products or services is continually updated by using organisational information

Feedback from customers regarding the products and services you offer are only worthwhile if you act upon them, especially if it is a problem relating to a new model which requires feedback to the manufacturer, as it could require a total recall of a range of vehicles.

Manufacturers rely on fast feedback from their retailers regarding a defect in a product or service so that they can institute a recall to ensure that consumers are protected and no one is injured due to the possible negligence.

1.2 Maintain service when systems go wrong

1.2.1 Reasons for failures in service are explained to customers immediately

There are many instances which can and do happen within organisations which affect Customer Services - telephone supply fails; three-phase electricity fails; cars get stuck on ramps; computer crashes; you are unable to source parts or to raise invoices or estimates; building has been evacuated due to fire or other emergencies.

While working in London I had 24 vehicles stuck up in the air due to electric failure; someone had cut through the power lines. Not only that, but the computers went down and we had lost a full day's keying of invoices, we were unable to locate parts on the computer or raise invoices.

When serious breakdowns occur it is crucial that the customers needs are catered for first and that they are informed immediately, either by telephone or fax. It would be worthwhile laying out a procedure to follow in the event of any failures such as those above.

I learned the hard way; we soon put in procedures to cater for those emergencies.

1.2.2 Customers are kept updated about interruptions in service

It should be understood that, while customers can be understanding regarding your problems, regular telephone contact should be made to reassure them of your interest in them and of the progress being made.

In our case, because we had contact telephone numbers, we were able to reassure all our customers that they would be kept mobile. It did mean we had to tax a few second-hand cars, and we had a big bill on the mobile phones, plus most of the staff had to stop back to produce invoices manually. And, when the electricity came back on, the technical team worked through the night to finish everyone's job. Then, of course, we had a day's re-keying to catch up on.

1.2.3 Information given to customers is designed to protect them from unnecessary worry

When you are in contact with customers, your communication with them should be designed to protect them from unnecessary worry. They should know that loan cars are available, that there is a collection and delivery service, and they should be reassured that you and your colleagues are doing everything possible to solve the problem. Stay calm and watch the tone in your voice; keep confident.

Without doubt our customers, while understanding our position, really wanted to know that we had not bumped their car and were trying to cover up while we repaired it. Believe it or not, several did come to see their car up in the air. It just goes to show that we have a long way to go to reassure the motoring public of our honesty.

1.2.4 *Service is maintained through unprompted extra efforts*

While it is difficult when systems go wrong to operate totally professionally, by using the brains of all your colleagues, and often through extra efforts, solutions can be found to cater for customers' needs. Certainly I could not have dealt with this major problem without the extra efforts of the employees owning the problem.

1.2.5 *Practical help is offered to colleagues to maintain service to customers when systems go wrong*

If the systems that go wrong do not affect your own operation, you should be encouraged to assist your colleagues to maintain service to customers, even if it was just collecting and delivering customers or cars. Constructive relationships with colleagues to foster team working has to play a major part in the future of our industry.

What I was most pleased with was that, in our emergency, the sales manager did not moan and groan about clean cars going out on loan or that there would be another name in the log book because we taxed the vehicle. This took immense stress off the service reception team and enabled them to handle the situation in a professional manner.

1.3 Maintain positive working relationships with colleagues

1.3.1 *Practical help is offered to colleagues under pressure in order to deliver service to customers*

Continuously look for improvements in your organisation's practices and procedures, discuss them with your colleagues, then document your ideas fully with designs, costs and the benefits both to the company and customers alike. Then present them to your team leaders; do not leave your brains at home, bring them to work with you.

For example: Customers coming to reception see three or four people behind the counter, one is a parts person, one is the warranty clerk, and one is the cost clerk. Unless they all have badges on indicating to the customers who and what they are, the customers assume that they are receptionists who are ignoring them. In any case, they should greet them quickly with a smile and indicate that they will get someone to attend to them.

1.3.2 *Own knowledge of product or services is continually updated through positive exchanges with colleagues*

While it is expected today that all team members are sales people, whether they are in parts, sales or service, it is important that each one of us looks after the customer's perceived needs. The customer with the high-mileage car who has not been to your company before needs to be questioned regarding their cambelt - has it been checked recently, do they understand that if it broke the repair costs could be over a thousand pounds? Especially if it had just been in for a small service with you, they would not be too happy with your organisation if faced with a large bill - and, in fact, may hold your company responsible, when it was not your fault.

This happened in one of my companies with the OFT and the RAC all involved. The dispute went on for weeks; my time alone sorting out the mess cost the company a fortune. Both the RAC and OFT suggested that, as we were the experts, we should have informed the customer and presented the option.

The poster illustrated opposite should be displayed in reception so that you can refer customers to it.

1.3.3 *Opportunities to improve working relationships with colleagues are consistently sought*

There is nothing worse than a customer coming to collect their car to find either that all the work has not been completed or it is not ready at the time promised.

This is one of the major complaints customers have today about the service we offer in our industry. Therefore, it is crucial that we continually monitor the progress of a customer's car, working closely with our parts

CUSTOMER ADVISORY NOTICE

CAMSHAFT DRIVE BELTS

Many vehicles today are fitted with flexible camshaft drive belts. Intervals for these to be changed vary according to manufacturer, but generally range between 36,000 and 70,000 miles.

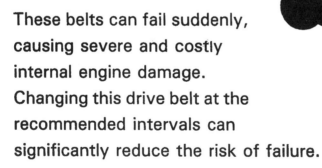

These belts can fail suddenly, causing severe and costly internal engine damage. Changing this drive belt at the recommended intervals can significantly reduce the risk of failure.

Ask us for the information regarding your vehicle, and for a quotation of the cost without any obligation.

Sample of customer advisory notice

and technical colleagues; and that we have procedures in place to notify customers of any delays in advance; and/or that we offer delivery/collection of their vehicle when it is complete.

The comment 'Sorry it's not ready yet as we are still waiting for parts' maybe gets you off the hook, but the customer thinks your company does not carry parts and this gives them negative feelings. Send them a Customer Satisfaction form and just see what comes back. It is you who got it wrong, not the parts department.

Having contacted your customer to inform them that we are unable to keep our delivery promise, it is important that your manager is alerted and informed, so that when the customer does come in the manager is aware and is able to respond to the customer's needs.

The customer at least will know that everything was being done to meet their expectations and that senior management was aware and a firm apology was forthcoming.

Making the customer feel welcome is nothing new. But if we are going to set ourselves apart from other retailers we must go further. Going further means being more than just polite. It's about creating a real sense of warmth; by always being there when needed, listening properly and attending to the customer's needs throughout their ownership of their vehicle - through: **PERSONAL ATTENTION; UNDERSTANDING; ACTING QUICKLY.**

1.3.4 *Own knowledge and experience of service systems is shared with others*

Some innovative companies in our industry whose managers ask and listen to members of their teams, and actively encourage team members to look at the gaps in the service given to customers, have come up with solutions to improve customer service and profitability.

It is all about you bringing your brains to work and not leaving them at home. You know the shortfalls in doing your job, such as leaving it to others to solve your problems, which affects you giving the best possible customer care, when really you, with some careful thought, could come up with a solution, and this solution, if documented and presented to your superiors in a professional way, would solve the problem.

1.3.5 *Co-operative work with others is used to deliver service to customers*

There will be times when you need to seek help and advice from others to solve customers' problems, such as whether a particular tow bar would fit their car or what weight the car would pull.

If you do not know the answer, the customer will always prefer you to find someone who does, rather than you waffle on or make up excuses. The skill is to ensure that the person whose assistance you are requesting understands the full extent of the customer's concerns, especially if they relate to technical know-how beyond your ability.

Be polite, introduce the customer to your colleague by name, and ensure that your customer understands you have introduced them to someone who will come up with the answers.

LEVEL 2 - UNIT 2

STORE, RETRIEVE AND SUPPLY INFORMATION

2.1 Maintain an established storage system

2.1.1 *New information is put into the storage system following organisational procedures*

Most companies spend thousands of pounds a year advertising to attract new customers and as much again in communicating with their own customer base.

It can cost as much as £10 per customer enquiry, so the importance of recording customers' names and addresses correctly every time you come in contact with them is crucial to the well-being of your company.

How many times does a customer ring in to say they have had a service reminder for a car they put in in part exchange with you months ago? Amending customer records and updating the relevant information shows professionalism.

Even if you are supplying parts retail on the front counter and the customer is paying cash, when giving them a receipt get their name and address, and the type of vehicle operated, so it can be added on to the computer base.

When ordering parts for customers, if the customer's details are not recorded correctly, they will get upset when we do not contact them at the time the parts come in, or worse still they do not come back at all and we are left with slow-moving stock.

In reception, how much aggravation is caused by a wrong chassis number in the voucher book, which is transferred to the job card, wrong parts ordered, rejected warranty claims, technicians wasting time at the parts back counter waiting for parts; or what aggravation if we have not got a contact number for authorization for additional work because we did not complete the job card in full (especially when it's a company car and we do not have the user's address and details).

2.1.2 *Stored material is maintained in good condition in the appropriate location*

Parts department often receive from the manufacturers superseded part numbers which, if not amended, create two part numbers for one part.

10

This can be costly since you could be ordering parts that you have already in stock, so it is crucial that the part numbers are updated regularly.

Menu price boards can quickly get out of date, as can times given for the job, which, if submitted wrongly in the case of warranty claims, causes rejection of the invoice. This will cause customer hassle if it is re-invoiced to them.

Checking and cleansing your customer data base on a regular basis is also important in ensuring that customers have not moved or changed their car. Postage today forms a major part of your company's expenses. You would be amazed at the number of gone-away service reminders that come back to the dealership after a mail shot.

2.1.3   *Item movements are monitored and recorded accurately*

When we have had to order a part specially for a customer's needs, either through VOR or TP, keeping track of when the part was ordered and when it arrives is crucial to your customer's needs. If you have made a promise to deliver by a certain date, it is imperative that you notify the customer immediately, either by phone or fax, when it has arrived or to tell them if you find it has gone on back order (the factory is temporarily out of stock).

Conway VAUXHALL — Viaduct Estate, Carlisle, Cumbria CA2 5BH, 0228-29401	WORKSHOP/INTERNAL "Top Priority" Order	ORDER NO: DATE COMPILED: DATE ORDERED:

ORDER TYPE:
PAGE NO:

PART NO. ORDERED	PART NO. SHIPPED	QTY.	ORDER STATUS	DESCRIPTION	CUSTOMER	ON FILE	FILE UP-DATED V.M. DETAILS	DATE DATE REC.	SIGN CHARGED ON	O R

COMMENTS: ADDED TO ORDER FILE: ORDER PLACED:

Sample of a Top-Priority Order

Failure to contact the customer results in them phoning several times and they lose confidence in YOU. This is a major cause of over-age stock, because the customer does not come back.

Most calls to customers during the day are usually bad news - more work needed or it will not be ready or one of the jobs cannot be done. So it is important to be well prepared before you make the phone call.

For example, if the car will not be ready at the agreed time we must say why it will not be ready and when it *will* be ready.

In the case of add-on work, we need to be precise on the details - why it needs doing, how much will it cost and how it will affect the collection time.

You should, if possible, sound concerned and sympathetic when you phone a customer with bad news, by using a warm friendly tone of voice; and try to be as helpful as possible.

2.1.4 Overdue items are identified and systems for return implemented

Much of the after-sales income in the future will rely on the older car coming in for service, so it is imperative that MOT reminders are sent out, and that the ones that do not come in are followed up. Having a system that updates vehicles gone away and indicates those that have been in and those that have not is important.

2.1.5 Out-of-date information is dealt with as directed

From time to time you may find mistakes in customer's records and without doubt it is your duty to own the problem. Things such as the customer driving about with the wrong registration number on the front of their car and the correct one on the back, or letters being addressed with the wrong initial, do upset customers, so we must be certain to amend customer files.

I experienced a very embarrassing situation when the husband of one of our customers had died and the family had informed us, but a member of the team forgot to amend the records. Needless to say, we kept sending out reminders for service and invites to test drives and open nights. The day I had to visit the lady with our company's apology was a sad day. You can be sure that from that day on procedures were put in place to make sure I never had to do that again.

A simple amendment form is shown on the facing page.

```
┌─────────────────────────────────────────────────────────────┐
│                CUSTOMER AMENDMENT FORM                       │
│  DETAILS _____│
│  _____│
│  _____│
│  _____│
│  _____│
│  _____│
│                                                             │
│  COMMENTS _____│
│  _____│
│  _____│
│  _____│
│  _____│
│  _____│
└─────────────────────────────────────────────────────────────┘
```

2.1.6 Opportunities for improving established systems are identified and appropriate action taken

Carved-in-stone practices of the past ('we have always done it this way') need to be continually improved. Often you are just the person to see that, instead of attaching four or five photocopy sheets to the back of the job card for the technicians or parts people to fill in, by just altering the information on the job card we could save hundreds of pounds in time and copy paper.

Attaching to the customer's keys a simple label showing where their car is parked can save the customer time in looking for their car.

It may be that some customers do not find our opening times convenient. How flexible are we in reviewing the services we offer and the way they are organised?

2.1.7 Work practices conform to organisational requirements

Have you ever had the customer who wanted you to use their own oil, or the one who wanted a cheap set of brake pads instead of the manufacturer's recommended ones? Your immediate response is, I suppose, to tell them it cannot be done. With this type of customer it is crucial that the customer is counselled by a senior member of your team, with an explanation that your work can only be guaranteed by using genuine parts, that, while you would be happy to carry out their instructions, you would have to insist that your disclaimer be documented on the invoice. That customer, if you turned them away, would tell everyone that you were a 'rip off' company. By you referring them to a senior member of your team, you showed you care about their needs.

2.2 Supply information for a specific purpose

2.2.1 Information requirements are understood

We all receive memos, sometimes from upstairs. They often do not look important to you; they could be related to loan-car usage, payment terms for customers or changes in organisational procedures.

However, your correct interpretation of this information and prompt action in implementing it can affect Customer Service.

For example, it may be that a recall has been announced, but by carrying out the checks on cars in the workshops today you will save customers having to come back in again.

I experienced an expensive problem when another garage contacted me to let me know about a couple who were using stolen cheques to pay for repairs and petrol. My memo went to all departments. However, the reception team were too busy to read not-another-Naylor memo. You guessed it, we were taken for £98. No bonus for reception team that month.

2.2.2 Information sources are correctly identified and accessed

If you do not have access to customer files for amendments, ensure that the information is passed on to the appropriate authority in a legible manner. If you make and design your own amendment document, customers can see that you care, by your writing the amendments down.

Another area which does need to be looked out for in the future is the use of postcodes. New computer software today is often designed in such a way that all you need to pull up customers' details is their post code, which gives their name and address, whether you have them on file or not. So start recording postcodes on all customers' records now.

2.2.3 Where available information does not match requirements, options and alternatives are identified and offered

It is important that information you receive from others within your organisation is acted upon promptly, such as the telephone message to ring a customer back, the part that is required from another retailer, the invoice that needs to be produced quickly, the estimate for fitting extras on a new car. All these, if not dealt with promptly, can affect Customer Service.

It is easy to use the old excuse that you do not have time; managing your time has to be a key skill that you must develop.

Sample of a customer history file up-date

To enable us to provide you with a quick and efficient booking in service and to
ensure our customer history file is up todate , it will be appreciated if
you will provide details as requested below and on the reverse side of this form.

We also take this opportunity to remind you to ensure that you bring the service
or warranty book with you when checking in the vehicle so , it can be duly stamped
when maintenance service is carried out.

	PERSONAL	COMPANY
NAME		
ADDRESS		
street		
town		
post code		
tele no		
mobile no		
pager no		
fax no		

VEHICLE DETAILS

REG NO		MAKE	
DATE REGISTERED		MODEL	
SELLING DEALER		ENGINE CAPACITY	
OWNERS NAME		ENGINE NO	
WORK CHARGEABLE TO		CHASSIS NO	
		DOOR KEY NO	
YOURSELF CASH		TRUNK KEY NO	
CREDIT		RADIO CODE	
CHEQUE		LOCKING WHEEL	
LEASE COMPANY; NAME		NUT KEY No	
COMPANY ACCOUNT		(key location)	
WARRANTY NEW VEH			
EXTENDED WARRANTY			
OTHER STATE DETAILS			

SPECIAL AUTHORIZATION

IN THE EVENT THAT ,WHILST CARRYING OUT WORK ON YOUR VEHICLE
IN LINE WITH YOUR INSTRUCTION, WE DETERMINE ADDITIONAL WORK IS REQUIRED.
CAN WE PROCEED WITH WORK UP TO A NET LIMIT OF :-

						PLEASE
£100	£150	£200	£300	£400	£500	CIRCLE

CUSTOMERS SIGNATURE.....   DATE..................

Over the years I have developed 14 ways to save time:
- Don't waste time regretting your failures.
- Don't waste your time feeling guilty about what you don't do.

- Examine old habits for possible streamlining; for example, revise carved-in-stone processes.
- Keep your watch three minutes fast, to get a head start on the day.
- Carry a notepad in your pocket to note down any ideas and reminders.
- Learn to skim read.
- Put signs up in your office reminding you of your goals.
- Always plan first thing in the morning and set priorities for the day.
- Keep a list of specific items to be done each day. Arrange them in priority order, and then do your best to get the important ones done as soon as possible.
- Do first things first.
- Train yourself to go down the to-do list without skipping over the difficult items.
- Set deadlines for yourself and others.
- Handle each piece of paper only once.
- Have a place for everything (so you waste as little time as possible looking for items).

2.2.4 *Information is correctly transcribed and compiled*

Customer service information, especially over the phone, needs to be conveyed professionally. Often customers ringing in do not understand that the person to whom they are speaking is only a parts person and therefore does not know the price for fitting, or, if they have the knowledge, the price book is not near the phone.

It is so important today that we get away from 'I am just parts' or 'I am just reception'. The customers want fast, accurate and reliable information, so the more knowledge you have of other people's jobs the more valuable you are to your organisation, and this, of course, improves the customer service you give.

2.2.5 *The information supplied is in an appropriate form*

Information that you pass on to others, such as the ordering of top priority parts, instructions to technicians and telephone messages, must be accurate, relevant and fully completed, so that the person who is receiving this information can carry out their function to a high standard.

The parts cannot be ordered correctly if the model number is only half complete.

When good specification of customer's concerns is passed on to the technicians, this enables the job to be done right first time.

I have seen instances where problems have arisen which could have affected customer care because the job card was made out as a diesel but the model number was for a petrol vehicle. The technician, when presenting the job card to the parts department, received a filter for a diesel. Needless to say, the technician passed their comments on to the parts person about their ability to do their job correctly. This then led to a fight on the workshop floor, which in turn led to two men being suspended from work. This placed extra pressure on the remaining staff to ensure all customers cars were completed as promised. All because the receptionist did not define the customer correctly and made assumptions that, because this customer's other vehicles were diesel, this one was.

The transferring of customers on the phone to different departments is so much nicer if you use the customers' names and pass on all relevant details so that customers do not have to repeat themselves over again.

2.2.6 *Essential information is supplied within required deadlines*

Especially in reception, customers who have a problem because they were not informed that their car would not be ready at the agreed time, or that the part had not arrived yet, or that it had but parts have sold it to someone else, really mark your organisation down hard on CSI standards which can cost your organisation thousands of pounds in bonus monies It is all about putting yourself in your customers' shoes. How would you feel?

2.2.7 *Confidential information is disclosed only to authorised persons*

There are laws relating to statutory obligations, called the Data Protection Act 1984. It would be wise to update yourself on this Act regarding stored information, since your company will need to be registered under the Act if you are storing any information other than a customer's name and address - for example, if you are building up a profile of a customer, such as their hobbies, number of children, their age, the type of work they do. You will need to be registered and operate under the Act's Code of Conduct. It is important that you do not leave information laying about on desks which can be used by criminals. For example, it would be easy for someone who has seen a job card with a name and address, registered number and key number for that person to get a key cut and steal one of your customer's cars.

The security of your customers' information must be strictly guarded.

Level 2 - UNIT 3

DEVELOP AND MAINTAIN POSITIVE WORKING RELATIONSHIPS WITH CUSTOMERS

This unit is made up of four elements, the first being:

3.1 Present positive personal image to customer

3.1.1 Treatment of customers is always courteous and helpful especially when working under pressure

The old saying 'you only get one opportunity to create a first impression' is so right. That is why, no matter how hard a day you have had, or what pressure you have been under, it is a part of your job to stay calm and collected when dealing with customers and working under stress.

Being able to recognise stress in yourself, and being able to deal with the causes of it, is a skill in itself. Only by identifying the causes can you make plans to eliminate them.

I found that I became stressed when I had not planned my day, or tried to do everything myself without delegating to others who were very capable.

I sometimes think that customer-facing people should look upon themselves as actors playing a part in the theatre. I am not suggesting that we should be insincere with people, as it is important that we should be ourselves. However, customers pay our wages and that long face and a sad tone in the voice can give our customers the wrong impression.

It really gives me immense satisfaction when customers either write in about a member of staff, congratulating them on a job well done or on how they handled the customer. If only we looked after customers every time this way, we would be on a winner.

3.1.2 Organisational standards for personal appearance and behaviour are consistently maintained

Personal presentation of yourself is probably the most difficult for any of your colleagues to pass comment on, as it causes embarrassment and even resentment should anyone have the nerve to comment.

Customers also will not comment - even if your hair is in a mess, there is dandruff on your shoulders, your tie is at half mast, your shoes are dirty, you have bad breath, body odour, white socks or bad personal habits such as picking your ears, nose, or teeth. But these things do put them off using your services, no matter how good you are at doing your job. So carry out a self-appraisal on a regular basis.

I had one 24-year-old service manager running a four-bay workshop. He was very good at his job, smashing with the customers, but would insist on wearing an ear ring and white socks. Nothing I could say or do would convince him to change his appearance. It was only when one day I received a letter from a satisfied customer commenting on how well he had been treated by the YTS laddie, that he changed his attitude towards his appearance.

3.1.3 Equipment and supplies used in transactions with customers are available, up-to-date and in good order

I suppose it goes without saying that when you want to use the photocopier it is out of paper or toner, or that we have just run out of loan car forms, or someone has used the last till roll and not bothered to order any more, or that we have run out of credit card vouchers, or the printer ribbon wants replacing, or we have run out of job cards.

All these things form part of our image to customers and, when it happens in front of them, we do feel embarrassed about it; yet we do nothing about it.

The key is for all the team to own a part of the problem. This way you will not be embarrassed and the customer gets service.

What action can you take to ensure your operation does not fall into an unacceptable category?

At one dealership that I was involved in, each of the team took on board a different area of the department. One looked after stationery, another the customer seating area, one even checked the loos for toilet paper. This really did solve the problem.

3.1.4 Opportunities for improving working relationships with customers are actively sought

There is little more important to a person than the use of their name. How do you feel when going into a public house and the landlord says 'Hello Mr...'? You feel good and comfortable with the situation. So the use of customers' names can develop trust; asking customers their suggestions of the services they would like that you currently do not offer also develops and improves working relationships.

Many companies today complete questionnaires and send out Rate-Our-Service cards. However, very few follow up or take any action.

Below is a typical Rate-Our-Service questionnaire that professional companies use and a sample analysis of the responses.

Dear Customer,

Complete customer satisfaction is always our aim. Whilst we make every effort to achieve this aim, your valued comments and observations on the service you have received from us today will ensure that we are successful in this endeavour.

I would be grateful if you would take a few moments of your time to complete this Questionnaire and post it to me.

Would you like to be contacted by any of the following:

Sales ☐   Service ☐

Parts ☐   Bodyshop ☐

Thanking you in anticipation of your assistance.

Customer Satisfaction Questionnaire

Please indicate your satisfaction with the items below by placing ☑ in one box for each item.

	Completely Satisfied	Fairly Satisfied	Dissatisfied
Ease in arranging an appointment?	☐	☐	☐
The time taken to attend to you in person?	☐	☐	☐
Offered an inspection of your vehicle before work commenced?		YES/NO	
Offered a Price Estimate?		YES/NO	
Attitude and efficiency of the Reception staff?	☐	☐	☐
Completion of all work requested?	☐	☐	☐
Work completed on time?	☐	☐	☐
Explanation of work carried out?	☐	☐	☐
Fairness of prices (if charged)?	☐	☐	☐
Cleanliness of vehicle on collection?	☐	☐	☐

ANALYSIS OF 'RATE OUR SERVICE' CARDS

PERIOD: NOVEMBER 1994

QUESTION	NUMBER OF RESPONSES	COMP. SATISFIED NUMBER / PERCENTAGE	FAIRLY SATISFIED NUMBER / PERCENTAGE	DISSATISFIED NUMBER / PERCENTAGE	REMARKS (When compared against October's Analysis)
Ease in Arranging an Appointment?	154 / 1st - 14	131 / 85.1% / 1st - 11 / 78.6%	18 / 11.7% / 2 / 14.3%	5 / 3.2% / 1 / 7.1%	Slight increase of 1.9% in the no. of Comp Sat customers but with an increase of 1.9% in Dissat customers (increased from 2 to 5)
The Time Taken to Attend to You in Person?	153 / 1st - 13	117 / 76.5% / 1st - 9 / 69.2%	30 / 19.6% / 1st - 4 / 30.8%	6 / 3.9%	Further decrease of 5.0% in Comp Sat (been decreasing since Aug's high) with an increase in Dissat of 0.5% (increased from 5 to 6)
Offered an Inspection of your Vehicle before Work Commenced?	99 / 1st - 12	YES / 32 / 32.3% / 1st - 5 / 41.7%	NO / 67 / 67.7% / 1st - 7 / 58.3%		Slight decrease of 0.7% in number of customers offered an inspection of their vehicle before work commenced
Offered a Price Estimate?	75 / 1st - 5	32 / 42.7% / 1st - 1 / 20.0%	43 / 57.3% / 1st - 4 / 80.0%		Slight increase of 1.0% in the number of customers who were offered a price estimate
Attitude and Efficiency of the Reception Staff?	155 / 1st - 13	132 / 85.2% / 1st - 13 / 100%	20 / 12.9%	3 / 1.9%	Decrease of 3.1% in the number of Completely Satisfied customers, with the number of Dissatisfied customers remaining fairly static
Completion of all Work Requested?	152 / 1st - 12	128 / 84.2% / 1st - 12 / 100%	13 / 8.5%	11 / 7.2%	Decrease of 1.4% in the number of Completely Satisfied customers, with an increase of 1.0% in Dissatisfied (increased from 9 to 11)
Work Completed on Time?	153 / 1st - 13	124 / 81.0% / 1st - 11 / 84.6%	17 / 11.1%	12 / 7.8% / 2 / 15.4%	Further decrease of 4.1% in number of Comp Satisfied customers with an increase of 1.7% in Dissat (increased from 9 to 12)
Explanation of Work Carried Out?	136 / 1st - 10	109 / 80.1% / 1st - 9 / 90.0%	16 / 11.8% / 1st - 1 / 10.0%	11 / 8.1%	Increase of 15.5% in number of Comp Satisfied customers but with an increase of 2.9% in Dissatisfied (increased from 5 to 11)
Fairness of Prices (if charged)?	66	42 / 63.6%	21 / 31.8%	3 / 4.5%	Decrease of 1.1% in number of Comp Satisfied customers, with a decrease of 2.8% in Dissatisfied (reduced from 5 to 3)
Cleanliness of Vehicle on Collection?	143 / 1st - 13	118 / 82.5% / 1st - 11 / 84.6%	19 / 13.3% / 1st - 2 / 15.4%	6 / 4.2%	Slight increase of 0.8% in Comp Satisfied but with a slight increase in Dissatisfied of 0.7% (increased from 5 to 6)
Other Comments	56 / 1st - 4	GOOD / 22 / 39.3% / 1st - 2 / 50.0%	BAD / 16 / 28.6% / 1st - 1 / 25.0%	OTHER / 18 / 32.1% / 1st - 1 / 25.0%	Received 209 responses in November 1993

22

3.1.5 *Own behaviour consistently conveys a positive image of the organisation to current and potential customers and to colleagues*

As I said before, the old saying 'you only get one opportunity to create a first impression' is so true. That is why, no matter how hard a day you have had, or what pressure you have been under, it is a part of your job to stay calm and collected when dealing with customers.

I used ten ways to increase my resilience to stress and make these suggestions:

- Analyse your individual stress situation and find out what keeps causing you trouble personally. Try to think how you might prevent these stress situations in future.
- If you can see no possibility of changing your individual situation, try changing your attitude.
- Do not take so seriously things which have annoyed you in the past.
- Compensate the stresses of the day by discussions or rewards on the same day.
- Try to anticipate a stress situation and adjust to it in good time.
- Relax completely at week-ends or on your days off, even if your ambition will not let you rest.
- Do not rely on your annual leave to act as compensation for stress. Your leave will bring new stresses and will not suffice as the sole means of compensation.
- Try to attain more emotional balance altogether. Do, for instance, use your leisure time for hobbies, sport etc.
- Physical reactions to stress (cardiac pain, sweating, circulatory trouble, stomach and intestinal trouble) are signals that must be taken seriously, and which make a consultation with your doctor imperative.
- Increase your self-confidence and try to adopt an optimistic attitude to life.

Every day you must adapt yourself to the stresses of your working environment, such as excessive work load, pressure of deadlines, unreliable fellow workers. Then again you may have to help out in an emergency, people bother and interrupt you, there may be too much noise, your colleagues are against you, the atmosphere at work is bad, you are passed over for promotion, and so on.

You cannot avoid these stress situations, but you can change your attitude to them.

3.2   Balance needs of customer and organisation

3.2.1   Determined attempts to meet customer needs are made within own limits of authority

Your own job description should outline the limits of your authority. However, often these are not well written and you need to clear with your superior the lines of communication for customer complaints - that is, who does what and when.

Today's innovative companies give authority as well as responsibility, enabling you to deal promptly and efficiently with customers' concerns.

How would you, for example, handle the customer who was not happy with their invoice, or the customer who had taken delivery of a used car two days ago and the exhaust had just fallen off. Do you have to go running to the sales manager for an order number; or do you check the customer's warranty and apologise, loan the customer a car without being asked for one and fit a new exhaust free of charge?

If you do the latter, you have a customer for life, who respects you and will tell all their friends of your company's no-quibble guarantee. If you keep them waiting while you telephone the sales manager for authority, argue with them about a loan car and suggest that the exhaust is not covered by warranty, you can be assured that customer delight will have just gone out of the window and the likelihood of them coming back again is slim. Remember customers pay our wages.

3.2.2   Organisational limitations are explained clearly and positively to the customer

To avoid customer dissatisfaction, it is crucial that they are informed right from the start as to what is to be done, how long it will take and how much it will cost; and you need to ensure that you know how they are going to pay.

3.2.3   All possible actions are taken to minimise conflict between customer needs and organisational limitations

It is amazing the number of customer complaints that revolve around paying the invoice - such as the cheque card only covering up to £100 (yet you knew that the bill would be over £100), or that the work shown on the invoice was not explained fully.

You can, by explaining fully your company's terms of doing business at the start, save a lot of hassle at the end, thus minimising conflict between customers' needs and your company's limitations.

One of the companies I worked with put in a procedure that all customers, when booking their vehicle in for repair or service, signed the job card confirming their agreement to the work being carried out, and at that stage were asked how they were paying - credit card, cheque, cash or on account. This eliminated hassle when the customer was collecting the vehicle and enabled the costing team to produce invoices in time for the customer to pay.

3.2.4 Organisational limitations are recognised and assistance sought from others

Companies have rules and regulations for a purpose and they have to be recognised and implemented by you. If by implementing these rules you come into conflict with a customer, do not argue. Just ask them politely if they would like to see your supervisor and reassure them that it is normal practice if the customer is not satisfied.

This would apply, for example, if a customer wished to take their car away without paying; or they wished work to be carried out under warranty when you knew that it was not covered.

3.2.5 Proposals put to customers are clearly recorded and stored in the appropriate place

It is good practice to record all that was said and agreed with a customer, either on the job card, on the invoice or under the customer's history file, so that in the event of disputes in the future others can handle the problem in your absence.

Most computer systems allow for additional remarks to be entered, but if not it is very important that a manual file is kept.

I have been in situations where customers have come back months after having a problem resolved by the offer of a free winter check, only to find that no-one knew anything about it, which put us back into a negative situation.

3.3 Respond to feelings expressed by the customer.

3.3.1 Customers' feelings are accurately judged through their
behaviour, tone, and through sensitive questioning

How customers feel when they come into your company can vary - they may be angry, distressed, vulnerable, or totally frustrated.

Your task is to identify quickly which one of these categories your customer might be feeling, either from the tone in their voice or from their behaviour through sensitive questioning.

'Next, where is your voucher book' is not the idea,

'Good morning, how can I be of service?' or 'How can I help you?' is more likely to get them to talk.

If you consider how you feel when everything has gone wrong at the start of your day - the alarm clock did not go off, you had a puncture on your way to work, you were cut up by another motorist, and finally when you got to work your colleague who had the keys to the office had gone sick - then you will understand that your customers can also have had a bad start to the day.

3.3.2 Customers' feelings are acknowledged and own behaviour
adapted accordingly

If a customer's car has just been run in to, they could be suffering anything from being angry to being totally frustrated and therefore will require sympathy, understanding and your total attention to their needs.

The customer bringing in their car for an MOT will no doubt feel vulnerable - 'Will it pass, if not how much will it cost to put it right?' They will require reassurance that it is for their and other road users' safety that their car will get the best check-over possible.

The key is to listen carefully, and give the customer your fullest attention. Eye contact is very important, and write down everything they say; use the person's name; show unquestionably that you respect and accept the person, regardless of race, sex, culture. More importantly, demonstrate respect for your colleagues and your company, as there is nothing worse than the employee who knocks their own company in front of customers.

3.3.3 Perceptions of customer's feelings are regularly checked with
customer

Body language will tell you a lot and will allow you regularly to check your customer's feelings. For example, head-and-eyes-down shows a negative attitude; head-tilted-to-one-side shows interest and approval; arms-folded-and-legs-crossed shows a defensive attitude.

The art of using body language when dealing with customers is well worth studying, since gestures and movements of the body all have a meaning which enable you to gauge what your customer is thinking.

3.3.4 *Relevant procedures are operated to respond to customers' complaints*

Customer complaints, or, more often than not, lack of understanding, need to be handled carefully, especially bearing in mind that it has cost the company a vast amount of money to get the customer to be our customer in the first place.

For example, how many times have we had a customer complain that their vehicle was damaged while in our care. They usually do this on the phone after they have taken the car away. You must get the vehicle back immediately to assess type and age of the damage (for your company's own defence).

This will show the customer that you are concerned about their complaint. However, express concern without admitting liability (eg 'I'm sorry to hear that Mr Hanley, please bring it in immediately so that we can have a look at it').

Another thing which can raise our hackles is the customer who comes in and complains that a small amount of money (small change for car parks) has been removed from their vehicle while it was on our premises. One possible response is to tell them that all personal effects are left in vehicles at the owner's own risk. You can imagine what effect this has on the customer. It will create the impression that you do not care that there may be thieves working in the dealership and stealing customers' property.

So it is important that you have a procedure to operate in the event of a customer complaint, either a Code of Conduct or company standing orders, which allows you to deal with and record what went wrong and to discuss with colleagues ways of ensuring it does not occur again.

Typical business Customer Service statistics show:
- Only 4% of dissatisfied customers will complain.
- 96% of those will go away quietly
- and of those 91% will never return.

Reasons why customers stop doing business with you:
- 1% die
- 3% move away

- 9% move for competitive reasons
- 68% because of an attitude of indifference from customer-facing employees, managers, switchboards and even dealer principals.

... and there are other important factors

- A dissatisfied customer tells on average eight to ten other people. One in five will tell 20 people.
- It takes 12 positive service experiences to equal one negative one.
- A typical company will spend six times more to get new customers than it does to keep existing ones.
- Low service quality companies get an average 1% return on sales and lose market share at 2% per year.
- High service quality companies get an average 12% return on sales and increase market share at 6% per year and they charge significantly higher prices.

Good Service
Brings
Rewards

3.4 Adapt methods of communication to the customer

3.4.1 *Appropriate types of communication are selected to keep customers informed about current or future actions*

There are many ways of communicating with our customers, face-to-face, telephone and the written word. In all cases, as well as the content, the tone of the communication is of immense importance.

This always applies - when carrying out telephone follow-ups after a customer has been in for service to ensure they were happy with the service; when notifying them that parts ordered for them have arrived in stock; when conveying service or MOT reminders; or when telling them that we have special offers on this month.

Without doubt, customers do like to be reminded from time to time that you value them as a customer and do not take them for granted.

3.4.2 *Written and spoken language is suited to the customer*

Choosing your words to suit the customer has to be considered and your language should be user-friendly, bearing in mind that customers do not understand motor trade slang or jargon. Speak slowly and try to have a smile on your face, especially on the phone. Keep your conversations short and to the point. Avoid the use of words like 'pal', 'mate', 'love', 'dear' or 'pet' - often these cause offence.

The same with written communications. The first sentence should attract them and make them want to read more. Again ensure that motor trade slang is not used.

3.4.3 *Methods of communication are suited to customers with individual needs*

Some of our customers may have impairments to their hearing or their speech, or have physical disabilities; some may speak with accents or dialects. Your skill in being able to respond appropriately to customers with individual needs is without doubt to be a professional.

The deaf do not have a problem if you give them paper to write on, or better still if you have learned sign language. You would be amazed how many extra customers would come to your company, as it soon gets about that you are a caring person.

Disabled drivers also require that little bit of extra attention. If you have ever pushed a wheelchair around the shops you will know what I mean.

However, just because they are not able-bodied does not mean that they need to be communicated with any differently. Speak to them in the same way as you would want to be spoken to yourself.

3.4.4 Understanding of communication is regularly checked with customer

To make sure that both we and the customer understand what we both want, care should be taken to ensure that we check regularly during our dealing with the customer, that we understand their special needs. We require patience if difficulties arise.

For example, it is not good practice to book a disabled person in at a time when the reception is going to be very busy and they would have difficulty in getting their wheelchair into the reception. Most companies who have disabled customers arrange special while-you-wait days.

3.4.5 Communication difficulties are openly acknowledged and appropriate help is sought to resolve them

When dealing with customers who fall into the special individual needs category, it may be that it requires a colleague also to be involved. Two heads are often better than one in these instances.

LEVEL 2 - UNIT 4

SOLVE PROBLEMS FOR CUSTOMERS

4.1 GATHER INFORMATION ON CUSTOMER PROBLEMS

4.1.1 *Customers' perceptions of problems are accurately identified and sensitively acknowledged*

Going on the defensive is a natural thing to do when customers complain, especially if the complaint relates to lack of parts or faulty workmanship. However, it is important that you listen carefully to your customers' comments to identify just what the complaint is about and that you acknowledge that you have understood what has been said. It is better if you write everything down.

4.1.2 *Customers' problems are clearly summarised using information gained from them*

All the time your customer is speaking to you, give them eye contact, show genuine interest, write everything down and summarise often to confirm that you understand fully, especially if you need to take the complaint to a higher level. There is nothing worse than a customer having to repeat themselves.

4.1.3 *Colleagues are consulted for information relating to problems affecting customers*

There will be times when you need to seek help and advice from others to solve customers' problems, such as whether a particular tow bar would fit their car or what weight their car can pull.

If you do not know the answer, the customer will always prefer you to find someone who does rather than you waffle on or make up excuses.

The skill is to ensure that the person whose assistance you are requesting understands the full extent of the customer's concerns, especially if they relate to technical know-how beyond your ability.

Be polite; introduce the customer to your colleagues by name; ensure that your customer understands you have introduced them to someone who will come up with the answers.

4.1.4   Recurring problems or complaints are recorded and passed to those who are in a position to provide solutions to them

Those companies which have achieved ISO 9002 will have a laid-down procedure for handling customers' complaints. If not, you should have at least a Code of Conduct to which you need to adhere. This enables you to be confident in assessing whether you have the authority to handle the complaint or need to pass it to a higher authority.

I found that having one person with authority who acted as a customer-care manager solved 80% of customers' complaints before they got out of hand.

4.2 Propose solutions for customers

4.2.1 *Assistance is sought from colleagues for solutions to customers problems*

While it is accepted that you like to solve all customers' problems, from time to time you may need to refer to others within your company, or to your zone manager representing the manufacturers, to bring the complaint to a satisfactory conclusion.

4.2.2 *Current organisational procedures are examined for solutions to customers' problems*

Often, while you have made every attempt to rectify and compensate the customer, they are still not satisfied. You can suggest to them that they may refer their complaint to the Office of Fair Trading (OFT).

However, you must ensure that you have made every effort and documented totally the customer's complaint and you must be prepared to abide by the OFT decision.

Most OFT offices, however, would welcome you calling them to discuss a possible customer complaint before you get into that situation. I have found that when you tell them what action you have already taken they will support you if they think the customer is being unreasonable. This can be very helpful as should the customer later go to the OFT they generally put the customer right. The OFT is there for all to seek advice from, companies and customers alike.

4.2.3 *Other products or services are proposed to solve customer problems*

The setting up of quality teams to carry out post-mortems on customer complaints is very important. By using the brains of all your colleagues, the development of new procedures can ensure that the complaints are not repeated.

For example, if we were for ever getting complaints about dirty steering wheels, say, or oil on the wings, it just could be that we do not have wing covers or hand towels in the right places within the workshops, or that our quality control needed to be sharpened up.

By just presenting the problem to the team responsible in a constructive manner you will find that they own the problem. If, on the other hand, you want to wield the big stick, I suspect that the problem will continue to occur.

4.2.4 *Proposals and reasons for them are understood by customers*

It is crucial, however, that action is taken on comments made by customers, as they soon get fed up with filling in questionnaires if no action is taken. So it is very important that the customer gets feed-back of action taken by your company. Even if resources do not allow you to do what your customers would like, they will know that you have listened.

4.3 Take action to deliver solutions

4.3.1 Standard procedures are promptly activated to deliver solutions to customer problems

As I have indicated in previous performance criteria, standard procedures often have been carved in stone over years. 'We have always done it this way' is the usual comment. But customers' needs are changing. They are expecting and demanding a higher and prompt service from you, so you must continually be looking for ways of improving your company's code of practice to keep up with the customers' needs and not leave it to your managers. You are at the sharp end and see and hear what customers are demanding.

For example, you might review some of the following points which can affect customers:

- Are the service or parts opening hours convenient for customers?
- Can customers get a fixed-time appointment for a job?
- Are customers offered a 'While you wait' service?
- Do we offer a collection and delivery service?
- Can customers get a loan car or hire car when their vehicles are in for service?
- Is the service reception area comfortable, with good lighting, heating and ventilation?
- Are there clean and comfortable seats for waiting customers, with no loss of place in a queue?
- Do we have a clean, well provisioned (paper, soap, towels) toilet available for customers?
- Is there any refreshment available, such as coffee or tea? Are there newspapers or television/videos to hold customer's interest while waiting for their vehicle?

These are just a few areas that can affect the customer care you offer.

4.3.2 Service delivery is checked and problems arising are passed to the appropriate authority

Some innovative companies in our industry, whose managers ask and listen to their teams and who actively encourage team members to look at the gaps in the service given to customers, have come up with solutions to improve customer service and profitability by forming innovation teams from all departments to discuss customers' concerns, from which discussions they have developed new procedures.

35

However, taking part in innovation teams can be a daunting task if you have not been involved in brain storming in the past.

The main rules of brain storming in groups are:

- Do not rise to speak.
- Keep your talks brief and on the problem.
- Be careful of the tone of your voice; speak in an easy conversational manner.
- Take up only one solution to the problem at a time.
- Support every solution YOU suggest with evidence that will help you put your point over. **Do not make claims.**
- Listen attentively to all speakers.
- Do not interrupt other speakers.
- If you disagree, ask questions of a speaker rather than making direct assertions. Do not argue.
- Write down everything in a predetermined manner.

4.3.3 Solutions to customer problems are carried out in co-operation with others

Handling customer complaints or problems is a skill that needs to be developed by all customer-facing personnel. Whether you are dealing with customers face-to-face, on the telephone or by letter or questionnaire, you must always tell the truth. Passing the buck or telling white lies will never solve the problem, especially if the end result is that you need to go to arbitration by recommending the customer to the OFT or Society of Motor Manufacturers and Traders (SMMT).

4.3.4 Action is taken, within own area of authority, to prevent shortfalls in the delivery of product or services

Together with your own records of customer feedback, you should look towards the trends or patterns in both your strengths and weaknesses. For example, customer care could fall down dramatically during staff holidays, or when key personnel are on sick leave. This is especially true at times of registration changes or the start of a new year when the volume of business is three times as much as normal. These are the times when you can get a poor result.

4.3.5 Action is taken to alert colleagues to potential shortfalls in the delivery of products or services

Other than the focus groups already mentioned in previous performance criteria, some retailers are carrying out exit polls. Talking to customers who are picking up their vehicles in the car park can give you an instant response as to how they feel they have been treated.

I conducted one of these exit polls and it was very surprising the comments given on our service. For example, most would have liked the reception team to have explained more fully the work which had been carried out for their bill of, say, £156.

Instead they were told how much it was, in a very pleasant manner. All courtesies were shown, but since when they get in the car they very often cannot see or feel any difference or benefit for the £156 just paid, they are sometimes left uncertain that any work had been done. Seeing them as they left did give me an opportunity of clarifying any uncertainties the customer may have had.

From this exit poll I was able to introduce a simple service check sheet (most companies have them but we were not using them) which would in future be signed off by the technician.

LEVEL 2 - UNIT 5

IMPROVE SERVICE RELIABILITY FOR CUSTOMERS

5.1 Respond promptly to the service needs of customers

5.1.1 Customer service needs are identified promptly and clearly

Customers today have high expectations of value for money and, because the media has not always been kind to us as an industry, customers are half expecting us to rip them off, and are indeed surprised if we give them a warm welcome to our company, maybe with a speedy acknowledging smile, that we keep our promises, that we use their name, and give them ours, that we explain fully our company's terms of doing business before we enter into a contract to supply them with our services.

We will always get the difficult customer but these are the challenges: - to win them over with that extra special attention and to exceed their expectations by responding quickly to their needs.

5.1.2 Delays are avoided through unprompted extra efforts

While we always expect those around us to operate at a high standard so that we can do our job, it is crucial that we 'check, check'. It was *you* who promised the customer that the car would be ready for five o'clock, and it is of no help when they come for the car and you say the parts department forgot to order the bits, because the customer was relying on *you*, not the parts department. Make every effort to 'check, check' so that you can keep the promises you make.

5.1.3 Current procedures are used flexibly to respond to the service needs of customers

It is important that you understand your company's standards and code of practice in dealing with customers, especially those who have a complaint. It is so easy to give in to the customer, which can cost your company hundreds of pounds. At the same time, if you dig your heels in and ignore your customer's needs, this also can cost the company hundreds of pounds in bad press. The skill is to put yourself in your customer's shoes. If it is a genuine complaint and is down to your company's incompetence or bad practice, then the customer should get action and compensation promptly.

5.1.4 Practical help is gained from others to respond to the service needs of customers

When compensation has been paid to a customer for poor service it is important that a full review takes place with all concerned to ensure that the problem is not repeated, and that it is documented and brought to senior manager's attention.

There are times when the complaint made does not relate to anything your company has done; for example, it could be that it is a manufacturing fault or a parts failure. It is so easy to abdicate responsibility. You should be firm but polite and take up the customer's complaint with your supplier or manufacturer, copying all your correspondence to the customer to show you care.

Without doubt, all manufacturers believe that their future lies in complete customer satisfaction and therefore, as a retailer of motor industry services, you must provide the highest level of customer service, since this leads to increased customer loyalty and ultimately increased profitability.

5.2 Use customer feedback to improve service reliability

5.2.1 Comments on service reliability are consistently sought from customers

Customer Satisfaction Surveys are here to stay in our industry and there will always be a certain amount of controversy surrounding these surveys, especially when your company's incentive programmes can be affected by poor reports from customers' feedback. However, asking the customers about the service experience they had with you allows you to assess your own performance - 'Am I being professional?'

5.2.2 Existing customer feedback procedures are actively used and outcomes reported regularly to the appropriate authority

Without doubt, you will be the first to know if your company has a bad Customer Satisfaction Survey, because it will have been drawn to the attention of the highest level within your company by your supplier. The skill is not to become paranoid about it, to use the reports constructively, to remember the customer is using this questionnaire to tell you something. Customers who have not had a good experience will ALWAYS fill it in, those who have an average experience will NOT fill it in, those who have had their expectations of their needs exceeded WILL fill it in.

5.2.3 Improvements to service reliability are initiated, within own area of authority, as a result of customer feedback

Most innovative companies today do not wait for their suppliers or manufacturers to carry out satisfaction surveys; they own the problem themselves, by regularly following up by telephone several days after the service has been given.

Questions need to be asked such as 'Were you greeted and served quickly?', 'Was all the work carried out that you asked for and was it explained in detail?', 'Did our team tell you about our special offers etc?', 'Did we fulfil all our promises'.

You will be amazed at how surprised customers are that you took the trouble to ask their opinion as to whether they were satisfied.

5.2.4 Colleagues are informed of service reliability improvements based on customer feedback

It is important that the feedback from customers, good and bad, is communicated to the whole team, in a constructive manner, and documented either in the vehicle or customer history file. It is also important that customers' comments are kept confidential, especially if they are critical of individuals. The skill is to turn negative comments into positive actions by ensuring the customers' concerns receive attention and acknowledgment from senior managers.

5.3 Work with others to improve service reliability

5.3.1 Ideas and experience of colleagues are used to improve reliability of own service

An apple cut in five slices from top to bottom and held together represents Sales, Service, Parts, Body Shop and Administration.

But what happens when we present the apple to the customer? It falls apart! If each department sees itself as self-contained, focused on its own targets and its own budget, there is no shared working relationships and no co-operation.

Are we condemned to this carved-in-stone way of thinking, or is there another way of slicing the apple (and naming the parts) so it holds together, with a shared core, enabling us to present a united front to the customer's needs?

Your ultimate goal has to be to use your skill and professionalism in motivating managers, colleagues and staff from other departments within your company, so as to present a united image towards your customer 'who pays all your wages'.

5.3.2 Improvements within own area of responsibility are communicated to others

Your job description, if written properly, should include a performance-related section, showing the results that are expected from you, and this should be reviewed every 12 weeks. For example, in reception we might be looking for 1800 hours sold per technician each year, or we may be looking at parts sold per labour hour of £35, or your department may be assessed on an After-sales Customer Satisfaction Survey, say, no lower than 75%. All these areas can be used to monitor both your and the department's progress towards customer satisfaction.

5.3.3 Current organisational procedures for service delivery are regularly evaluated with colleagues

Your relationship with other departments within your organisation must be of a high standard so that requests for help to meet customers' needs are met promptly. The day you need an extra loan car from sales it needs to be forthcoming without the usual moans and groans. Your skill in being able to coerce co-operation from others to the benefit of the customer is paramount.

Being on good terms with your manufacturer's warranty departments often enables you to obtain goodwill gestures for your customers and creates the image that you care, which develops loyalty from the customer.

Customers are most in need of help and attention when they contact you in emergencies. So it is vital to provide a high standard of service. What if one of your customers phones in with a breakdown, from a long way away? What should you do?

Still take the problem off his hands. Do not tell him to phone the nearest dealer. You should do it, then phone the customer to tell him what arrangements you have made for him.

The skill is having the correct attitude towards your fellow man.

5.3.4 Action is taken to alert others to changes in procedures needed to improve service reliability

Identifying the company's weaknesses from Customer Satisfaction Surveys, and Rate-Our-Service questionnaires, and then doing something about them, will benefit customer care.

5.3.5 Outcomes of co-operative work with others are actively used to improve service reliability

Bench-marking against best-practice retailers will also enable you to compare your performance, by using composites created by your supplier, such as Tracker, Inter Firm Comparisons (IFC), BM90, MIDAS. We are so lucky to have this information, but it is often never shared with the team, for reasons of confidentiality. If you do not see this information, reassure your managers that you are a responsible person. It will enable you to look for new ideas to improve your performance.

For example, would you know that the average hours sold per technician was around 1850 per annum, or that the average parts sold per labour hour sold was £39, or that the average parts person sells £130,000 of parts per annum at cost.

The key is to assess what your competitors are doing better than you, then improve your performance to beat them.

INTRODUCTION TO CUSTOMER SERVICE
LEVEL 3 UNITS

Key Purpose: **DELIVER CONTINUOUS IMPROVEMENT IN SERV-ICE TO ACHIEVE CUSTOMER SATISFACTION**

Customer Service Level 3 has five main units. Within these units are 16 elements, which have 84 performance criteria which have to be met.

This NVQ is ideal for senior receptionists, master technicians, senior parts persons.

As in the previous units, when you get your portfolio do not panic. Your assessor will take you through it step-by-step. Just read it through several times, looking at the performance criteria required for each element.

Several of the performance criteria contained in the units in Level 3 are the same as in units contained in Level 2, so the explanation of knowledge required will be the same.

LEVEL 3 - UNIT 1

MAINTAIN RELIABLE CUSTOMER SERVICE

This unit is made up of three elements, the first being:

1.1 Maintain records relating to customer service

1.1.1 Documentation is comprehensive, is correct in detail and contains relevant facts

Most companies spend thousands of pounds a year advertising to attract new customers and as much again in communicating with their existing customer base.

It can cost as much as £10 per customer enquiry, so the importance of recording customers' names and addresses correctly every time you come in contact with them is crucial to the wellbeing of your company.

How many times does a customer ring in to say they have had a service reminder for a car they gave in part exchange with you months ago? Amending customer records and updating the relevant information shows professionalism.

Even if you are supplying parts retail on the front counter and the customer is paying cash, when giving them a receipt get their name and address and the type of vehicle operated, so it can be added to the computer base.

When ordering parts for customers, if the customer's details are not recorded correctly, they get upset when we have not contacted them when the parts have come in. It would be worse still if they did not come in at all and we were left with slow-moving stock.

1.1.2 Facts are set out clearly and concisely

In reception how much aggravation is caused by a wrong chassis number in the voucher book, which is transferred to the job card, wrong parts ordered, warranty claims rejected, technicians' time wasted at the parts back counter waiting for parts; or the aggravation when we have not got a telephone number to ring for authorization of additional work, because we did not complete the job card in full (especially when it is a company car and we do not have the user's address and details).

1.1.3 Records are regularly and accurately checked and up dated

Parts departments often receive from the manufacturers superseded part numbers which, if not amended, create two part numbers for one part. This can be costly, as you could be ordering parts that you have already in stock. It is crucial that these are updated regularly.

Menu price boards can quickly get out of date, as can times given for the job, which if submitted wrongly in the case of warranty claims causes rejection of the invoice, causing customer hassle when the job is re-invoiced to them.

Checking and cleansing your customer data base on a regular basis is also important, ensuring that customers have not moved or changed their car. Postage today forms a major part of your company's expenses, you would be amazed at the number of gone-away service reminders that come back to the company after a mail shot. If these addresses are not deleted from the customer file, the costs will increase.

1.1.4 Suggestions for the improvement of record systems are clearly based on customer needs

As computer systems are becoming more and more widely used, and new software is being introduced, it is important that, as front-line team members, we continually look for improvement of our own systems, which are based on our customers' needs.

One example is that the vehicle history should have a key number and radio code included, so that we can produce it in the event of the customer needing this information urgently, or indeed our own technicians needing it if the battery has been disconnected and they have to restore the radio to a working condition. (Some diagnostic machines can find this information when connected to the management system of some cars).

1.1.5 Suggestions for the improvement of customer service record systems are suitably delivered to the appropriate authority

Many companies operate different systems, but it is important that you ensure that *your* system is fully maintained, so as to produce service and MOT reminders or, say, reports of customers who have not been in for service in the last 12 months.

Often computers are set up by the accountants, who are more concerned about the accounts than about what the system can do to improve customer care. So, if you do not know everything about your system, ask and you may find it is not being used to its full extent.

For example, if your computer has a report-generator facility it can be programmed to produce all sorts of valuable information, such as a list of all cars due next month for an MOT (assuming that we put the date first registered on the system when it was set up). Already we can see how important correct updating of the system can be in affecting your customer care.

1.1.6 Records which can be used to monitor service delivery are clearly identified

Rate-our-service cards are often used by companies. It is a good idea to get the technicians to place these in the cars themselves, as it focuses their mind on doing the job right first time. It enables you to monitor come-back jobs against each technician, as well as to pass on the compliments.

1.1.7 Records can be retrieved easily by others

Customer details or vehicle-history details form a very important part of a company's business, since they provide the information used to answer customers' most frequent emergencies - generally, the lost key number or radio code. It is essential to be able to get that information quickly, without those lengthy phone calls to the factory. And the vehicle service history is, of course, essential to the technician working on a regular customer's car.

1.1.8 Records conform to relevant statutory obligations and requirements regarding confidentiality

There is a law relating to statutory obligations as regards stored information, called the Data Protection Act 1984. It would be wise to update yourself on this Act as your company will need to be registered under the Act if you are storing any information other than a customer's name and address; for example, if you are building up a profile of a customer including things such as their hobbies, number of children, their age or the type of job they do. You will have not only to register, but also to operate under the code of practice laid down. It is important that you do not leave laying about on desks information which can be used by criminals. For example, it would be easy for someone who has seen a job card with a name, address, registration number and key number for that person to get a key cut and steal one of your customer's cars.

It is easy to see why security of your customers' information must be strictly controlled.

1.2 Organise own work pattern to respond to the needs of customers

1.2.1 Advice is sort when limits of own authority and competence are recognised

Have you ever had the customer who wanted you to use their own oil, or the one who wanted a cheap set of brake pads instead of the manufacturer's recommended ones? Your immediate response is, I suppose, to tell them it cannot be done. With this type of customer it is crucial that they are advised by a senior member of our team, with an explanation that our work can only be guaranteed by using genuine parts and, while we would be happy to carry out their instructions, we would have to insist that our disclaimer be documented on the invoice. That customer, if you turned them away, would tell everyone that we were a 'rip-off' company. By you referring them to a senior member of our team, you show you care about their needs.

1.2.2 Practical help is sought assertively to maintain service to customers during peaks in your own work load

First thing in the morning and last thing at night, you have to be well organised, especially in service receptions and parts back counters.

Innovative companies have developed new processes to ease the load, enabling customers to be looked after promptly during these busy times. One way, for example, is making the job cards up the night before; another is by pre-picking parts for those job cards or obtaining order numbers from fleet operators the night before.

It is a good idea to encourage salespeople to get involved in meeting and greeting customers in the morning, especially if there is a queue at reception.

The skill is your ability to coerce others to serve the motoring public to everyone's benefit.

1.2.3 Practical help is offered to colleagues to maintain service to customers during their workload peaks

Without doubt, the beginning of the month, with new cars going out and used ones coming in, is a busy time for the sales teams. Bearing in mind that these could also be service department's new customers in the future, getting involved in handovers, demonstrations, and used-vehicle appraisals will bring you into contact with new and potentially-new customers. Getting involved at this time can often cement a relationship to the future benefit of the company.

1.2.4   Delays are avoided through unprompted extra efforts

Sitting in on a sales meeting will often give you an indication of forthcoming work loads especially if the sales team have had a good weekend. Just knowing that you had four alarms to fit in two days, before the job card was raised, would help both you and the customer to ensure delivery dates were met.

The parts team, working closely with reception and sales, can pre-order non-franchise parts required the next day for used cars and customers alike, instead of waiting for the technician to present the job card in the morning.

It is all about questioning the customer at the time of booking the vehicle in and getting as much information as possible, especially on the telephone. It is also about communicating with your sales colleagues, who are often able to use such information to advantage in initiating future sales.

1.2.5   Positive efforts are always made to meet abnormal and unexpected work loads

The importance of keeping up to date with WIP (Work In Progress) invoicing, especially at month-ends, is crucial. Delays in invoicing warranty claims, spending on internal work and financing credit customers can have a dramatic effect on the company's cash flow.

Parts team also must respond to sending back exchange units on time to ensure surcharges are reclaimed and not lost. Stock orders which come in late should be booked in quickly so that VOR (Vehicle Off the Road) jobs can be processed immediately and customers can be contacted regarding TP (Top Priority) orders.

All these urgent work loads cannot always be done between 8am and 6pm. If you respond to these work loads by working beyond your normal hours of work, customer delight will be ensured, *and* you will be recognised by your managers as a professional.

1.2.6   Plans to meet the known demands of future workloads reflect the benefits of experience

One of the main problems which is often raised within motor retailers is the communication between departments, especially sales, service and parts, around the July-August time, when currently we do a third of our year's sales in one month.

Unless, knowing the units (that is, the number of vehicles) to be sold, we plan to have all the accessories in stock that the sales team will need, the sales team will not feel like selling them. They will not want the aggravation of handing over a unit incomplete. If the service department is not fully staffed during July and the first two weeks in August for used-car preparation, again customer care and our own work loads will get out of hand.

Profits do not just happen they are planned, planned by professionals.

1.2.7 Own ideas and experience respond senistively to team and customer needs

As an individual you need to assess where you are going and how you are to get there.

You need to look at your ideas. They may be controversial and they may include many different tasks and objectives. However, start with the simple things, the ones that are the easiest to achieve but which will have the most impact on customer care and, of course, on your department's bottom line.

Share your ideas - to feel involved, people need to know what's going on and why it is going on. Consult with your colleagues, invite their ideas, ask what their needs are. Often the best solution is arrived at through using the brains of every one; a joint effort is shared ownership.

1.3   Work with others to benefit the customer.

1.3.1   *Opportunities to improve working relationships with colleagues are consistently sought*

An apple cut in five slices from top to bottom and held together would represent Sales, Service, Parts, Body Shop and Administration.

But what happens when we present the apple to the customer? It falls apart! If each department sees itself as self-contained, focused on its own targets and its own budget, there is no shared working relationships and no co-operation.

Are we condemned to this carved-in-stone way of thinking, or is there another way of slicing the apple (and naming the parts) so it holds together, with a shared core, enabling us to present a united front to the customers' needs?

Your skill and professionalism in motivating managers, colleagues, and staff from other departments within your company to work at presenting a united image towards your customer, 'who pays *all* your wages', has to be your ultimate goal.

1.3.2   *Current organisational procedures for monitoring service delivery are regularly evaluated with colleagues*

Your job description, if written properly, should include a perform-ance-related section, showing the results that are expected from you, and this should be reviewed every 12 weeks. For example, in reception we would be looking for 1800 hours sold per technician each year, or we may be looking at parts-sold-per-labour-hour of £35.

Or your department may be assessed on an After-sales Customer Satisfaction Survey, say, no lower than 75%. All these areas can be used to monitor both your and the department's progress towards total customer satisfaction.

1.3.3   *Communications with relevant outside parties are effectively maintained on behalf of customers*

Your relationship with other departments within your organisation must be of a high standard so that requests for help to meet customers needs are met promptly. The day you need an extra loan-car from Sales, it needs to be forthcoming without moan and groans. Your skill in being able to command co-operation from others to the benefit of the customer is of paramount importance.

Being on good terms with your manufacturer's warranty departments often enables you to obtain goodwill gestures for your customers. This reinforces the image that you care, which encourages loyalty from the customer.

Customers are most in need of help and attention when they contact you in emergencies. So it is vital to provide a high standard of service. What if one of our customers phones in with a breakdown, from a long way away? What should you do?

Still take the problem off their hands. Do not tell them to phone the nearest dealer. You should do it, then phone the customer to tell them what arrangements you have made for them.

The skill is having the correct attitude towards your fellow man.

1.3.4 New contacts likely to benefit customer service are routinely identified through routine scanning of relevant information

Identifying the company's weaknesses from Customer Satisfaction Surveys, and Rate-Our-Service questionnaires, and then doing something about them will benefit customer care.

Shown here is a Customer Satisfaction Performance summary, such as is produced by some companies.

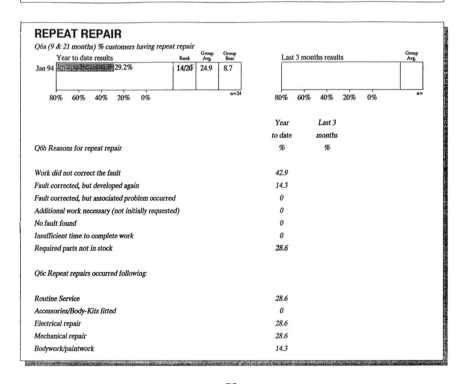

CUSTOMER SATISFACTION PERFORMANCE

REPEAT REPAIR

Q6a (9 & 21 months) % customers having repeat repair

Year to date results	Rank	Group Avg.	Group Best
Jan 94 29.2%	14/20	24.9	8.7

80% 60% 40% 20% 0%   n=24

Last 3 months results   Group Avg.

80% 60% 40% 20% 0%   n=

	Year to date %	Last 3 months %
Q6b Reasons for repeat repair		
Work did not correct the fault	42.9	
Fault corrected, but developed again	14.3	
Fault corrected, but associated problem occurred	0	
Additional work necessary (not initially requested)	0	
No fault found	0	
Insufficient time to complete work	0	
Required parts not in stock	28.6	
Q6c Repeat repairs occurred following:		
Routine Service	28.6	
Accessories/Body-Kits fitted	0	
Electrical repair	28.6	
Mechanical repair	28.6	
Bodywork/paintwork	14.3	

Becoming involved in the local TEC's Investment in People programme will develop all the team to work together towards customer service.

1.3.5 Collaborative work with others is actively used to improve the reliability of service delivery

Bench marking against best-practice retailers will also enable you to compare your performance by using composites supplied by your supplier, such as Tracker, Inter Firm Comparisons (IFC), BM90, MIDAS. We are so lucky to have this information, but it is often never shared with the team, for reasons of confidentiality. If you do not see this information, reassure your managers that you are a responsible person. It will enable you to look for new ideas to improve your performance.

For example, would you know that the average hours sold per technician was around 1850 per annum, or that the average parts sold per labour hour sold was £39, or that the average parts person sells £130,000 of parts per annum at cost?

The key is to assess what your competitors are doing better than you then improve your performance to beat them.

The sample of a Service Composite Report shown on the next page will indicate how the results of everyone's efforts can be brought together and analysed.

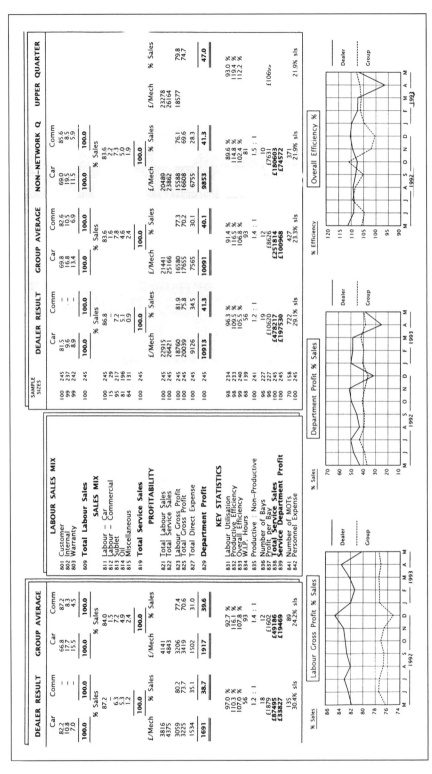

Sample of a Service Composite Report

LEVEL 3 - UNIT 2

COMMUNICATE WITH CUSTOMERS

This unit is made up of three elements, the first being:

2.1 Select information for communication to customer

2.1.1 Relevant documentation is routinely examined for information relevant to customers

Most computer systems today enable after-sales to select reports which can routinely supply information relevant to customers' needs, such as MOT reminders, service reminders and when they last visited the company.

While customers do not always like unsolicited mail, they do like to know when their MOT is due.

2.1.2 Customers' perceptions of problems are accurately identified, checked and acknowledged in all communications

Cars are a very emotional product and often, as we all know, customers perceive a problem and become paranoid. The skill in handling this type of customer is to show that we have checked and identified their concerns and to communicate this to them in a way that acknowledges their concern; and then to reassure them that you have investigated everything.

One way of doing this, for example, is, if the customer is having difficulty in defining their car's problems, to get from them a complete description, at the same time to show interest and concern and to show that you treat their problem seriously. So you do not 'put words into the customer's mouth'.

To be able to convey clear instructions to the workshop, we need to listen carefully and to ask questions to clarify the symptoms. Concentrate on defining the symptoms of the problem clearly, not the possible solution.

Many customers complain that receptionists use technical 'jargon' by asking customers what is wrong, rather than telling them. Try to phrase your questions so that they do not include technical words.

Often by asking the customer 'Can you say what it sounds like?' or 'When does it occur?' or 'Does it occur at particular speeds?' you can lead the customer to explain themselves better.

2.1.3 Information given in response to customer requests meets their needs in terms of accuracy, relevance, promptness and completeness

Our industry is its own worst enemy when it comes to giving customers a written estimate or quotation for a job. It is so important that information is given to customers quickly and is accurate. The use of menu price boards or pre-printed quotation forms helps immensely in meeting the customer's needs.

We should always give the customer the total price that they are to pay - that is, labour plus parts and VAT. Then the customer is not surprised by the total figure when the bill is presented.

Your aim must be to ensure no nasty surprises when the customer receives their bill.

2.1.4 Customers are promptly told about products or services which meet their identified needs

Customer details or Vehicle History details form a very important part of a company's business, since those details are used to satisfy customers' needs, provide the lost key number or the lost radio code, to trigger the MOT reminder. If the details are not set up correctly in the first place (often by the salesperson or sales admin) this can and does affect Customer Service.

Incorrect instructions on job cards to the technician can also cause poor communication, which can result in customer hassle, especially if it is a problem job and the vehicle has been in before for the same job. This often can be solved by attaching to the job card a copy of the service history, on the assumption, of course, that the information is complete on the history file.

(See also the situation and comments under Level 2, Performance Criteria 1.3.3)

2.1.5 Information given to customers is presented in a way which minimises worry

From time to time manufacturers recall vehicles for modifications. If it is your job to follow these up, especially with second-owner vehicles, it is important that you watch the tone in your voice. Be reassuring and well prepared regarding the recall programme; explain fully the implications.

2.1.6 *Information of potential use to customers is stored in the most appropriate place*

As pointed out in previous performance criteria, the two most called upon bits of information requested by customers is the radio code and the car key number. These should be stored on the vehicle history file, enabling the whole team to have access. However, for security purposes you must verify that the customer is who they say they are.

At this point, it may be worth mentioning that customers usually want this information over the telephone and it is impossible to over-emphasise the importance of the impression which you convey to a caller during the first few seconds of the call. During these vital few seconds the customers are making their assessment of your company; and once they have made up their mind, it will be very hard to make them alter their impression later.

Some dos and don'ts when answering the telephone:
* Answer every call promptly - when busy, answer politely and ask the caller to hold, don't let it ring.
* Speak clearly.
* Be bright, cheerful and enthusiastic.
* Don't eat or smoke while you are on the telephone; the customer needs your full attention.
* Choose a businesslike greeting. I recommend: 'Good morning/ afternoon. It's Bill Naylor speaking. How can I help you?'
* Don't fall into the trap of a 'sing song' greeting as it does not sound sincere.
* Don't use words such as 'mate', 'yeh', 'OK' and 'right then'. 'Yes certainly' and 'of course, sir' are much better tools to use.

Your business will increase and customer care will improve if calls are dealt with correctly.

2.2 Improve the flow of information between organisation and customer

2.2.1 Information given to and drawn from the customer is within a timescale acceptable to them

GOD GAVE US TWO EARS AND ONE TONGUE. PERHAPS HE WAS TRYING TO TELL US SOMETHING.

Careful defining of a customer's needs is essential at all times. For example, the customer who is just wanting an engine tune and adjustment of the brakes could, in fact, have a full service for the same price, covering all the items on the menu price board. Sensitive questioning and careful listening can establish analysis of opportunities for future customer service, especially if it is a new customer.

2.2.2 Communication optimises the customer's time

While we have all met the customer who wants to chat all day, most are in a hurry, either to get a lift or to get to work. Your company code of conduct for response times in acknowledging customers as they enter your department must be met. Assess the feelings of your customer. Are they angry, distressed, vulnerable or frustrated? Take an interest in what the customer is saying; give them your undivided attention; indicate interest by maintaining contact with your eyes and by the expression on your face; ensure that you get all the information you require by two-way communication. Managing your time, and that of your customers, especially at peak periods, is a skill worth developing.

2.2.3 Existing opportunities and procedures for communicating with customers are promptly used

In our industry, it is especially after-sales procedures for communicating with customers that are not always taken seriously. Service reminders, MOT reminders, telephone satisfaction follow-ups, rate-our-service follow-ups, parts-in-stock follow-ups, special offers, all play an important part in developing customer care.

The retailers who treat this part of their business with a high priority are the ones who are giving the most professional customer care and, combined with marketing of all your company's services in a controlled manner, this will present the right image cost effectively.

Your skill is to use all the procedures available to you, ensuring that the content, quality and timing are regularly monitored.

For example, if you know that a particular month is very quiet for service-hours sold, a mail-shot to customers whose cars are more than three years old, offering with every service a free MOT, can bring customers in early. In June, for instance, you could drag forward all the cars which are due for MOT in July, that is, the August deals of three years previous, bearing in mind that nearly a quarter of all cars need their MOT at this time.

2.2.4 New opportunities for communicating with customers are developed and used on appropriate occasions

Often we introduce new services and cannot understand why they do not work, such as all-day Saturday and Sunday working in after-sales, or late-night opening.

Innovative companies have introduced Focus Groups, made up of customers and potential customers, which meet every four months with you to discuss, not what you want, but what they want. Asking the motoring public how they want to be served gives you a better chance of developing new services which work.

2.2.5 Identified customer problems are discussed with colleagues who are in a position to influence potential solutions

Innovative companies within the motor industry tend to set up quality teams, made up of members from all departments, which, by using the brains of all the team members, solve and recommend to their management action to be taken to improve customer care.

It was found that if these teams were set up by individuals themselves, who understood the workings of their operations on a day-to-day basis, they were able, by members communicating with each other, to make not only improvements to customer care but also reduce the day-to-day hassle involved in their own job function.

For example, one company I worked with established that many of their customers who did not use them for service started work at a local factory at 6am in a morning and finished at 4pm. By offering loan cars to be collected at 5pm each night, customers were enabled to bring their car in for service the night before. What then happened was that other customers asked for this special service as they did not want to queue up on a morning.

We then brought in an evening shift to work 4pm to 9pm. This enabled these customers to collect their car in the morning and return the loan car, giving us better use of our loan cars since we could use them during the day for short loans and, of course, for demonstrations.

It takes a bit of thinking about, but changing carved-in-stone policies to suit the customers' needs does work.

2.3   Adapt methods of communication to customer.

2.3.1   *Appropriate communication media are selected to keep customers informed about current or future actions*

There are several ways of communicating with our customers, mainly by face-to-face conversation, by telephone and by the written word. In all cases, the tone of the communication is of immense importance, as well as the content.

We may be carrying out telephone follow-ups after a customer has been in for service to ensure they were happy with the service. A good way of doing this is by saying:

'We are reviewing our customer care programme and, as you had your vehicle in for service, were you satisfied with the way you were handled? Was your car ready when promised? Did we explain the invoice to you and carry out all the work requested? Is there anything you feel we could have done better?'

It is very important that you give the impression that you value their opinion, and just a small follow-up letter, thanking them for their time and noting their comments, is always appreciated.

Notifying customers that parts ordered for them have arrived in stock, sending them service or MOT reminders, telling them that we have special offers on this month - all are important and can be communicated to the customer by phone, postcard or letter.

Without doubt, customers do like to be reminded from time to time that you value them as a customer and do not take them for granted.

2.3.2   *Written and spoken language is suited to the customer*

Choosing your words to suit the customer has to be considered. Your language should be friendly, bearing in mind that customers do not understand motor-trade slang or jargon. Speak slowly and try to have a smile on your face, especially on the phone. Keep your conversations short and to the point. Avoid the use of words like 'pal', 'mate', 'love', 'dear' or 'pet'. Often these cause offence.

It is the same with written communications. The first sentence should attract them and make them want to read more, again ensuring that motor-trade slang is not used.

Postcards containing a short message are cost-effective when used to inform customers, such as letting them know we have ordered parts for their car. Giving customers a receipt for the work on their car, especially when collecting or delivering vehicles, is always appreciated.

Two simple ideas are shown here. If you do not like these, then change them, but use something.

Boleyn Docklands
South Crescent
Cody Road
London E16 4TL

Telephone: 071-511 4754
Facsimile: 071-511 4693

Dear Customer,

While carrying out the service and repairs to your vehicle

Reg. No. .... , we have found it necessary to order

a part specially from Vauxhall Motors.

As soon as the required part arrives, we will contact you to arrange fitment.

Should you at any time wish to check progress,
please telephone our
SPECIAL DIRECT LINE on 071-511 0694
and ask for our Parts Manager.

8/92 PT1

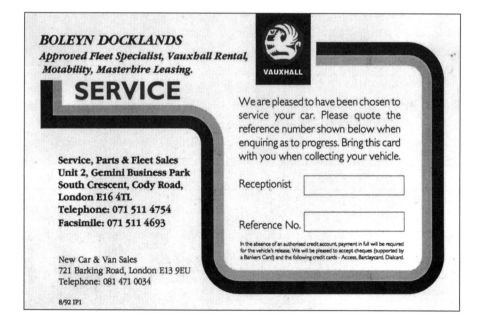

BOLEYN DOCKLANDS
Approved Fleet Specialist, Vauxhall Rental,
Motability, Masterhire Leasing.

SERVICE

We are pleased to have been chosen to service your car. Please quote the reference number shown below when enquiring as to progress. Bring this card with you when collecting your vehicle.

Service, Parts & Fleet Sales
Unit 2, Gemini Business Park
South Crescent, Cody Road,
London E16 4TL
Telephone: 071 511 4754
Facsimile: 071 511 4693

Receptionist

Reference No.

In the absence of an authorised credit account, payment in full will be required for the vehicle's release. We will be pleased to accept cheques (supported by a Bankers Card) and the following credit cards - Access, Barclaycard, Dialcard.

New Car & Van Sales
721 Barking Road, London E13 9EU
Telephone: 081 471 0034

8/92 IP1

2.3.3 Methods of communication are suited to customers with individual needs

Some of our customers may have impairments to their hearing or speech, or may have physical disabilities. Some may speak with accents or dialects. Without doubt, to be a professional you must use your skill to respond appropriately to customers with special needs

Disabled drivers also require extra attention. If you have ever pushed a wheel chair around the shops, you will know what I mean.

However, just because they are not able-bodied does not mean that they need to be communicated to any differently. Speak to them in the same way as you would want to be spoken to yourself.

2.3.4 Understanding of communication is regularly checked with customer

To be certain that both we and the customer understand what we both want, care should be taken to ensure that we check regularly during our conversation with the customer, ensuring that we understand their special needs and have patience if difficulties arise.

For example, it is not good practice to book a disabled person in at a time when the reception is going to be very busy and they would have difficulty in getting their wheelchair into the reception. Most companies who have disabled customers arrange special while-you-wait days.

2.3.5 Communication difficulties are openly acknowledged and appropriate help is sought to resolve them

It may sometimes be that it requires a colleague to be involved, as two heads are better than one in those instances when we are dealing with customers who fall into the special-needs category.

Many companies which operate Motability Schemes have a specialist who is trained to handle these customers' needs. It may be that your customers should book their cars in with this specialist, especially if the car came from your company in the first place.

One of my own companies created a special section to cater for special-needs customers, covering everything from clothes, wheel chairs, special attachments and open days. It was amazing how, by word of mouth, each customer recommended us to their friends; so much so that we were supplying up to ten cars a month, which guaranteed us the servicing and, when monitored carefully for condition, gave us good-quality used-car stocks after three years.

LEVEL 3 - UNIT 3

DEVELOP POSITIVE WORKING RELATIONSHIPS WITH CUSTOMERS

This unit is made up of three elements. The first is:

3.1 Respond to the needs and feelings expressed by the customer

3.1.1 Customer's needs are identified promptly, clearly and sensitively

Customers today have high expectations of value for money and, because the media has not always been kind to us as an industry, customers are half expecting us to 'rip them off'. They are indeed surprised, therefore, if we give them a warm welcome to our company, maybe with a speedy acknowledging smile, and if we always keep our promises, use their name all the time and give them ours, and finally if we explain fully our company's terms of doing business before we enter into a contract to supply them with our services.

We will always get the difficult customer but this is the challenge: to win them over with that extra special attention and to exceed their expectations by responding quickly to their needs.

For example, do we set out our customers' bills in a way that is easy for them to understand? Are all the different items of work listed separately?

It is important to show that we have carried out all the work that the customer requested. If a customer queries anything on their bill, how can you show that you are concerned to help them? You do so by listening and not interrupting, being patient, being honest, and not inventing answers. Seek clarification of anything you are unsure about.

3.1.2 Customers' feelings are accurately gauged through observation of their behaviour, tone, and through sensitive questioning

How customers feel when they come into your company can vary from being angry, distressed, vulnerable, to being totally frustrated.

Your task is to identify quickly which one of these categories your customer is feeling, either from the tone in their voice, or their behaviour through sensitive questioning.

'Next, where's your voucher book' is not the idea. 'Good morning, how can I help you' is more likely to get them to talk.

I have found that, no matter how much training you have, communicating with customers comes from experience. You should consider yourselves as a football team. They practice between themselves each week so that, when they go out to play the competition, they *perform* as a team. It would do us good to practise between ourselves one night a week to perfect our customer care routines.

Remember that the customer in front of you feels as if they are going into hospital. 'Will you find anything wrong, will you have the cure, will I be out tonight?' they wonder. It is preferable if we say: 'Try this and if it's not any better in a week, come back and see us.' How often have we heard that said at the doctors?

Sensitive questioning and checking of what the customer wants is so important. The usual 'Next have you got your voucher book' has no place in today's customer care approach, but it still goes on - not, however, with professionals.

Customers have statutory rights and therefore it is important that, when discovering customers' needs, we are careful of what we say. Without knowing it, we could commit our company to a verbal contract, which could have expensive consequences if we were unable to fulfil their needs.

3.1.3 Own behaviour is always adapted to the perceived needs and feelings of the customer

If a customer's car has just been run into, they could be suffering from feeling angry to being totally frustrated. They will require sympathy and understanding - and they will require your total attention to their needs. You will need to take control of the problem, reassure them and give them confidence that you will take care of their pride and joy.

The customer bringing their car in for an MOT will no doubt feel vulnerable. 'Will it pass, and if not, how much will it cost to put right?' They will require reassurance that it is for their own and other road users' safety that their car will get the best check-over possible.

The key is to listen carefully and give the customer your fullest attention. Eye contact is very important and write down everything they say.

It is a great help, too, if the person dealing with the customer has at their fingertips all the information available. Useful sample forms to be completed by non-reception staff are shown overleaf.

SERVICE BOOKING IN FORM   (SECTION 1)

DEAR CUSTOMER .

To enable us to provide you with a quick and efficient booking in service and to
ensure our customer history file is up todate , it will be appreciated if
you will provide details as requested below and on the reverse side of this form.

We also take this opportunity to remind you to ensure that you bring the service
or warranty book with you when checking in the vehicle so , it can be duly stamped
when maintenance service is carried out.

	PERSONAL	COMPANY
NAME		
ADDRESS		
street		
town		
post code		
tele no		
mobile no		
pager no		
fax no		

VEHICLE DETAILS

REG NO		MAKE	
DATE REGISTERED		MODEL	
SELLING DEALER		ENGINE CAPACITY	
OWNERS NAME		ENGINE NO	
WORK CHARGEABLE TO ;-		CHASSIS NO	
		DOOR KEY NO	
YOURSELF CASH		TRUNK KEY NO	
CREDIT		RADIO CODE	
CHEQUE		LOCKING WHEEL	
LEASE COMPANY; NAME		NUT KEY No	
COMPANY ACCOUNT		(key location)	
WARRANTY NEW VEH			
EXTENDED WARRANTY			
OTHER STATE DETAILS			

SPECIAL AUTHORIZATION

IN THE EVENT THAT ,WHILST CARRYING OUT WORK ON YOUR VEHICLE
IN LINE WITH YOUR INSTRUCTION, WE DETERMINE ADDITIONAL WORK IS REQUIRED.
CAN WE PROCEED WITH WORK UP TO A NET LIMIT OF :-

PLEASE

£100   £150   £200   £300   £400   £500   CIRCLE

CUSTOMERS SIGNATURE.....   DATE...................

Sample customer info update form to be used by non-reception staff

SERVICE BOOKING IN FORM   (SECTION 2)

PLEASE COMPLETE THIS SECTION ,CLEARLY DEFINING SERVICE WORK REQUIRED

SERVICE   (please circle)

SMALL
FULL

ENGINE PROBLEMS   (please circle)

POOR STARTING		MISS FIRE	HESITATION
COLD	LIGHT THROTLE	ONE PASSENGER	NORMAL EXHAUST
HOT	FULL THROTLE	FULL LOAD	WHITE EXHAUST
			BLUE EXHAUST

DRIVE LINE PROBLEMS   (please circle)

LIGHT LOAD	SPEED _____	DRIVING STRAIGHT
HEAVY LOAD	GEAR _____	CORNERING
		BRAKING

RATTLES   (please circle)

FRONT	ENGINE AREA	SPEED
REAR	EXHAUST SYSTEM	GEAR

ITEMISE HERE WORK REQUIRED

CAR CARE PRODUCTS

Check out our parts ,accessories and car care products which are available to our service customers at very special prices ,for example look at these unbeatable deals :-

WD 40 £##   A/FREEZE £##   S/WASH £##   V/OIL £##

(please circle)

CUSTOMERS SIGNATURE.....   DATE....................

Sample service booking-in form to be used by non-reception staff

3.1.4 Perceptions of customer needs and feelings are regularly checked with customer

Body language will tell you a lot and will allow you regularly to check your customer's feelings. For example, *head-and-eyes-down* shows a negative attitude, *head-tilted-to-one-side* shows interest and approval, *arms-folded-and-legs-crossed* shows a defensive attitude.

The art of using body language when dealing with customers is well worth studying. Gestures and movements of the body all have a meaning which enable you to gauge what your customer is thinking.

For example, how do you tell a customer whose car has been in the workshop all day that no fault was found because the symptom did not occur while the vehicle was in the workshop? How do you think the customer feels?

They will be concerned, annoyed that they will have to continue experiencing the fault. Watch their body language. While they may not say anything, you can be sure their body and facial expressions will tell you everything.

Possible suggestions could be:

- Leave the car with us, for our service manager to take home tonight to try and detect the problem.
- Ask the customer to make notes about the next time it happens, with things to look out for - was the engine hot or cold, what type of driving, what type of road, were you braking or accelerating?
- Offer the customer the opportunity of going out with the tester or foreman to point out the symptoms.

However, no-fault-found problems often originate from the customer not being questioned sufficiently or listened to properly when the vehicle was booked in.

3.2 Present positive personal image to customer

3.2.1 Treatment of customers is always courteous and helpful especially when own circumstances are under stress

The old saying 'you only get one opportunity to create a first impression' is so true. That is why, no matter how hard a day you have had or what pressure you have been under, it is a part of your job to stay calm and collected when dealing with customers.

I have discovered ten ways to increase resilience to stress:

- Analyse your individual stress situation and find out what keeps causing you trouble personally. Try to think how you might prevent these stress situations in future.
- If you can see no possibility of changing your individual situation, try changing your attitude.
- Do not take so seriously things which have annoyed you in the past.
- Compensate the stresses of the day by discussions or rewards on the same day.
- Try to anticipate a stress situation and adjust to it in good time.
- Relax completely at weekends or on your days off, even if at other times your ambition will not let you rest.
- Do not rely on your annual leave to act as compensation for stress. Your leave will bring new stresses and will not suffice as the sole means of compensation.
- Try to attain more emotional balance altogether. Do, for instance, use your leisure time for hobbies, sport etc.
- Physical reactions to stress (cardiac pain, sweating, circulatory trouble, stomach and intestinal trouble) are signals that must be taken seriously, and which make a consultation with your doctor imperative.
- Increase your self-confidence and try to adopt an optimistic attitude to life.

Every day you must adapt yourself to the stresses of your working environment, such as excessive work load, pressure of deadlines, unreliable fellow workers. Then again you may have to step in in an emergency, people bother and interrupt you, there may be too much noise, your colleagues are against you, the atmosphere at work is bad, you are passed over for promotion and so on.

You cannot avoid these stress situations, but you can change your attitude to them.

Wherever possible I tried to deal with stress situations on the same day, and often it worked. So don't sleep on it; sort it out, discuss it with a friend today.

I sometimes think that customer-facing people should look upon themselves as actors playing a part in the theatre. I am not suggesting that we should be insincere with people as it is important that we should be ourselves. However, customers pay our wages, and that long face and a sad tone in the voice can give our customers the wrong impression.

3.2.2 Standards for appearance and behaviour are consistently maintained

Personal presentation of yourself is probably the most difficult thing for any of your colleagues to pass comment on, as it causes embarrassment and even resentment should anyone have the nerve to comment.

Customers will not comment if your hair is a mess, there is dandruff on your shoulders, your tie is at half-mast, you have dirty shoes, bad breath, body odour, white socks, or bad personal habits such as picking your ears, nose, or teeth. But these things do put customers off using your company's services, no matter how good you are at doing your job. So carry out a regular self appraisal.

3.2.3 Equipment and supplies used in transactions with customers are available, up-to-date and in good order

I suppose it goes without saying that when you want to use the photocopier it is out of paper or toner, or that we have just run out of loan-car forms, or someone has used the last credit card voucher and not bothered to order any more, or that the printer ribbon wants replacing or we have run out of job cards.

All these things form part of our image to customers, and when it happens in front of them we do feel embarrassed about it, don't we?

The key is for all the team to own a part of the problem. This way you will not be embarrassed and the customer gets a prompt service.

Take whatever action you can to ensure your operation does not fall into the category of un-remedied problems.

3.2.4 Opportunities for improving working relationships with customers are actively sought

Many companies today send out questionnaires and rate-our-service cards, but very few follow up or take any action. If you do, you will improve your working relationships with customers.

I found that, by getting a senior member of staff to write to customers thanking them for taking the time to respond to our questionnaires, customers were made to feel important and were made aware that we valued their opinion.

3.2.5 *Own behaviour consistently conveys a positive image of the organisation to current and potential customers*

There is nothing more important to a person than the use of their name - how does a man feel when going into a public house and the landlord says 'Hello, Mr...'?

He feels good and comfortable with the situation. In a similar way, by using customers' names, *you* can develop trust.

Asking customers their opinion of the services they would like that you currently do not offer also develops and improves working relationships.

3.3 Balance the needs of customer and organisation

3.3.1 Persistent attempts are made to meet customer needs

Your own job description should outline the limits of your authority. However, often these are not well written, so you need to clear with your superior the lines of communication for customer complaints; that is, who does what to whom and when.

Today's innovative companies give authority as well as responsibility, enabling you to deal promptly and efficiently with customers' concerns.

How would you, for example, handle the customer who was not happy with their invoice, or the customer who had taken delivery of a used car two days ago and the exhaust had just fallen off? Do you have to go running to the sales manager for an order number, or do you check the customer's warranty details and apologise, loan them a car without them asking for one, and fit a new exhaust free of charge.

If you do, you have a customer for life, who respects you and will tell all their friends of your company's no-quibble guarantee. If you keep them waiting while you telephone the sales manager for authority, argue with them regarding a loan car and suggest that the exhaust is not covered by warranty, you can be assured that customer delight will have just gone out of the window and the likelihood of them coming back again is slim.

Service reception job-descriptions should always have a section which outlines in detail what results you are responsible for and also what authority you have.

You will have some major responsibilities for results, whether it is hours sold, workshop loading, work in progress or CSI performance results. All these should be documented in figures so that your performance can be measured.

At the same time you should also know what over-all authority you have and this can be split into three sections: financial, personnel, operational

Financial:
- What discounts can you give on labour and parts without seeking permission?
- How much are you authorised to give on a credit note?
- Can you authorise a free loan car?
- Can you authorise abnormal warranty claims?
- Do you have authority for capital expenditure - for example, the

workshop electric drill has packed up; can you get another or do we have to wait for a board meeting?

- Do you have authority to authorise overtime so that a rush job can be completed?

Personnel:
- Do you have authority over the drivers or cleaners?
- Can you ask them to do collection and deliveries?
- If you have people reporting to you, such as a cost clerk, can you discipline them, or recommend them for training, or even recommend a salary increase for them?

Operational:
- Are you responsible for the opening and closing of the department?
- Do you have responsibility for the maintenance of equipment?
- If so, to what monetary level can you authorise?

If you had the authority for all these things, would it improve customer care within your company?

3.3.2 *Options for mutual gain are identified and all relevant parties are clearly informed*

While it is important that manufacturer's warranty terms are not abused, items which could be claimed on warranty should be brought to the customer's attention, especially when the warranty is about to expire.

For example, I had paid for a new set of brake discs on my Toyota Supra. After 5000 miles the car started to judder. While discs and brake pads are subject to normal wear and tear and not always subject to warranty, my dealer changed them free of charge because he was aware that there had been a batch of faulty discs and he could submit them under warranty. My delight was that I had not purchased the first set from him but he still looked after me, using information that I could not possibly have known about.

3.3.3 *Options for mutual gain are cost effective for both parties*

While abnormal warranty claims can be a lot of trouble - getting authority, doing the paperwork etcetera - it is our responsibility to make every effort to ensure that our customers have every opportunity to receive payment for items which are genuinely abnormal failures.

By supplying me with new discs and pads, my faith in the Toyota product increased and my respect for the service receptionist who took the trouble to fill out all the forms and make a claim on my behalf was very high. More importantly, I told all my friends and colleagues about the experience.

3.3.4   Organisational limitations are explained clearly and positively to the customer

To avoid customer dissatisfaction, it is crucial that they are checked right from the start as to what they want, and that they know how long it will take and how much it will cost. And you need to ensure that you know how they are going to pay.

3.3.5   All possible actions are taken to minimise conflict between customer needs and organisational limitations

It is amazing the number of customer complaints that revolve around paying the invoice - such as finding the cheque card only covers up to £100 yet you knew that the bill would be over £100, or that the work shown on the invoice was not explained fully.

By explaining fully your company's terms of doing business at the start, you can save a lot of hassle at the end, minimising conflict between customers' needs and your company's limitations.

One of the companies I worked with put in a procedure that all customers, when booking their vehicle in for repair or service, signed the job card confirming their agreement to the work being carried out. At that stage they were asked how they were paying - by credit card, cheque, cash or on account. This eliminated hassle when the customer was collecting the vehicle and enabled the costing team to produce invoices in time for the customer to pay.

3.3.6   Flexibility in your organisational limitations is thoroughly explored and own proposals confirmed with others

Companies have rules and regulations for a purpose and they have to be recognised and implemented by you.

If by implementing these rules you come into conflict with a customer, do not argue. Just ask them politely if they would like to see your supervisor and reassure them that it is normal practice if the customer is not satisfied.

For example: maybe our opening hours are not suitable for the customer to collect their car; or that we don't accept a particular credit card; or that the customer wishes to take the car without paying.

3.3.7 *Outcomes of proposals put to customers are clearly recorded, stored and relayed to the appropriate personnel*

It is good practice to record all that was said and agreed with customers either on the job card, invoice or under the customer's history file, so that, in the event of disputes in the future, others can handle the problem in your absence.

Most computer systems allow for additional remarks to be entered, but if not it is very important that a manual file is kept.

I have been in situations where customers have come back months after having a problem resolved by the offer of a free winter check, only to find that nobody knew anything about it, which put us back into a negative situation.

35 WAYS TO AVOID FRICTION... WITH CUSTOMERS

1. Be where the customer expects to find you.
2. Greet, or at least acknowledge the customer's presence, quickly.
3. Have competent assistance to help when you are not available.
4. Don't dress in bad taste.
5. Take care of your personal appearance and hygiene.
6. Open relationships quickly, through smile and name exchange.
7. Believe that everybody is a BUYER until they prove otherwise.
8. Always get information from customers as soon as possible.
9. Keep your desk or work area neat and tidy.
10. Lead the customer by controlling the conversation.
11. Find out about the customer's requirements.
12. Find out about the customer's needs.
13. Show interest in what the customer is saying.
14. Don't show little or no interest in the customer's feelings.
15. Write down details including follow-up information.
16. Never be over-familiar with customers.
17. Don't talk too 'glibly', indicating a lack of sincerity.
18. Don't smoke in front of customers (unless the customer decides to smoke first).
19. Never 'knock' a customer's car or competitors.

20. Don't involve 'jargon' when talking to customers.
21. Don't make tactless remarks.
22. Make sure that your product knowledge is up to date.
23. Don't set out to impress yourself rather the customer.
24. Don't pretend to know the answer to questions when you don't.
25. Don't make false claims regarding your service or product.
26. Never apologise for the price of your product or services.
27. Don't leave the customer alone, unless it is really necessary.
28. Don't offer tatty or dog-eared literature.
29. Always thank customers for their business.
30. Never break a promise to a customer.
31. Always adopt a united front with customers.
32. Never 'pass the buck'.
33. Leave personal problems behind you when you go to work.
34. Remember customers represent profit while you remain a company overhead.
35. Always remember the two lies that you can tell to customers: YOU ARE RIGHT; IT'S MY FAULT.

LEVEL 3 - UNIT 4

SOLVE PROBLEMS ON BEHALF OF CUSTOMERS

This unit is made up of three elements. The first is:

4.1 Identify and interpret problems affecting customers

4.1.1 *Customers' perceptions of problems are accurately identified and sensitively acknowledged*

Going on the defensive is a natural thing to do when customers complain, especially if the complaint relates to lack of parts or faulty workmanship. However, it is important that you listen carefully to your customer's comments so that you can identify just what the complaint is about. Acknowledge that you have understood what has been said and write everything down.

4.1.2 *Information relevant to customers' problems is gathered and systematically analysed and prioritised*

All the time your customer is speaking to you, give them eye contact, show genuine interest, write everything down and summarise often to ensure you understand fully, especially if you need to take the complaint to a higher level. There is nothing worse than customers having to repeat themselves.

4.1.3 *Customers' problems are clearly summarised using perceptions and information gained from them*

Check that solving the customer's problem is within your authority and that it is a genuine problem.

Without doubt, a sincere apology helps to establish constructive relationships with the customer. Watch the tone in your voice as customers soon can take offence.

As a dealer principal I have had some real hot-tempered customers to deal with and I found from experience that the key was to listen intently. If we had caused the problem, or there was reasonable doubt that we could have caused the problem, I would immediately agree with them, that I would be just as annoyed as they were if it had happened to me.

Often you can take the steam out of the customer's complaint by ensuring that they have immediate use of a loan vehicle; or offering a free service or valet can restore their confidence in both you and your company.

4.1.4 Responses are designed to protect customers from unnecessary worry

It is important that, in the event of customers' vehicles being recalled by the manufacturer, they are reassured that every effort is being made to ensure that they are not inconvenienced; for example, by offering loan cars, or a collection and delivery service.

Recall campaigns are very important, especially if safety related, and, while very time-consuming, your customers expect you to let them know quickly. They do not like to see it in the press first. They need you to have solved the problem before their friends start passing comment.

Be aware of the full facts; do not pass the buck; watch the tone of your voice; and stay calm.

4.2 Generate solutions on behalf of customer

4.2.1 *All relevant complaints procedures are examined promptly for effective solutions to customer problems*

Those companies which have achieved ISO 9002 will have a laid-down procedure for handling customers' complaints. If not, you should have at least a code of conduct which needs to be followed. This enables you to be confident in assessing whether you have the authority to handle the complaint or whether you need to pass it to a higher authority.

I found that having one person with authority who acted as a customer-care manager solved 80% of customers' complaints before they got out of hand.

4.2.2 *Advice is sought from relevant sources for effective solutions to customer problems*

There will be times when you need to seek help and advice from others to solve customers' problems, such as whether a particular tow bar would fit their car or what weight their car will pull when towing.

If you do not know the answer, the customer will always prefer you to find someone who does, rather than you waffle on or make up excuses.

The skill is to ensure that the person whose assistance you are requesting understands the full extent of the customer's concerns, especially if it relates to technical know-how beyond your ability.

Be polite, introduce the customer to your colleagues by name and ensure that your customer understands you have introduced them to someone who will come up with the answers.

4.2.3 *Current procedures are flexibly interpreted to generate solutions which benefit customers*

While it is accepted that you like to solve all customers' problems, from time to time you may need to refer to others within your company, or the zone manager representing the manufacturers, to bring the complaint to a satisfactory conclusion.

4.2.4 *Alternative solutions are identified which benefit the customer*

When you have made every attempt to rectify and compensate the customer and they are still not satisfied, you can suggest to them that they may refer their complaint to the Office of Fair Trading (OFT).

However, you must ensure that you have made every effort and documented totally the customer's complaint - and be prepared to abide by the OFT decision.

Most OFT offices, however, would welcome you calling them to discuss a possible customer complaint before you get into that situation. I have found that, when you tell them what action you have already taken, they will support you if they think the customer is being unreasonable. This can be very helpful as, should the customer later go to the OFT, they generally put the customer right. The OFT is there for all to seek advice from, companies and customers alike.

4.2.5 *Potential new procedures are identified, explored and agreed with appropriate colleagues*

The setting up of quality teams to carry out postmortems on customer complaints is very important. By using the brains of all your colleagues, new procedures can be developed which will ensure that the complaints are not repeated.

For example, if we were for ever getting complaints about dirty steering wheels or oil on the wings, it just could be that we do not have wing covers or hand towels in the right places within the workshops, or that our quality control needed to be sharpened up.

By just presenting the problem to the team responsible in a constructive manner, you will find that they own the problem. If, on the other hand, you want to wield the big stick, I suspect that the problem will continue to occur.

4.3 Take action to deliver solutions

4.3.1 Procedures are promptly activated to solve customer problems

As I have indicated in previous performance criteria, standard procedures often have been carved in stone over years. 'We have always done it this way' is the usual comment, but customers' needs are changing. They are expecting and demanding a higher and prompt service from you, so you must continually be looking for ways of improving your company's code of practice to keep up with the customers' needs, and not leave it to your managers. *You* are at the sharp end and see and hear what customers are demanding.

For example, you might review some of the following points which can affect customers:

- Are the service or parts opening hours convenient for customers?
- Can customers get a fixed-time appointment for a job?
- Are customers offered a 'While you wait' service?
- Do we offer a collection and delivery service?
- Can customers get a loan car or hire car when their vehicles are in for service?
- Is the service reception area comfortable, with good lighting, heating and ventilation?
- Are there clean and comfortable seats for waiting customers, with no loss of place in a queue?
- Do we have a clean, well provisioned (paper, soap, towels) toilet available for customers?
- Is there any refreshment available such as coffee or tea; are there newspapers or television/videos to hold customer's interest while waiting for their vehicle.

These are just a few areas that can affect the customer care you offer.

4.3.2 Clear information about recurring problems and complaints is promptly passed to targeted individuals

Some innovative companies in our industry, whose managers ask and listen to their teams and actively encourage team members to look at the gaps in the service given to customers, have come up with solutions to improve customer service and profitability and they have developed new procedures by forming innovation teams from all departments to discuss customers' concerns.

However, taking part in innovation teams can be a daunting task if you have not been involved in brain storming in the past.

The main rules of brain storming in groups are:
- Do not rise to speak.
- Keep your talks brief and on the problem.
- Be careful of the tone of your voice; speak in an easy conversational manner.
- Take up only one solution to the problem at a time.
- Support every solution YOU suggest with evidence that will help you put your point over. DO NOT MAKE CLAIMS.
- Listen attentively to all speakers.
- Do not interrupt other speakers.
- Instead of making direct assertions, ask questions of a speaker if you disagree. Do not argue.
- Write down everything in a pre-determined manner.

4.3.3 Clear information about effective solutions is promptly passed to targeted individuals

It is all about you bringing your brains to work and not leaving them at home. You know there are shortfalls in doing your job, leaving it to others to solve your problems, which affect you giving the best possible customer care, when really you, with some careful thought, could come up with a solution, which, if documented and presented to your peers in a professional way, would solve the problems.

When I try up and down the country to create innovation teams from all departments of a dealership, my first hurdle is that staff tend to say they are not paid to think, or that if they come up with ideas the management do not listen, or they say 'We tried that and it did not work'.

The key is for you to imagine that it is *your* company *your* money. What would you do differently? And do not say sack the managers, as often they are just as frustrated as you are, because their boss treats them the same way. However, if we are to become the most profitable customer-care dealership, using the brains of all the employees is the secret.

4.3.4 Delivery of solutions is monitored and suitably modified to resolve any problems arising

Most franchised retailers are monitored by their suppliers, through Customer Satisfaction Surveys (CSS). However, it is important that you carry out your own rate-our-service surveys, either by telephone follow-ups or questionnaires left in the vehicles.

These follow-ups need to be carried out with some sensitivity as customers, especially those who mistrust our industry, may think that something is wrong with the work that you have carried out. Reassure them that you are looking for their input to improve the service you offer.

4.3.5 Appropriate media are used in all communications with customers

While the telephone and questionnaires are generally fine to collate information, the best-practice format is customer-focus groups where you are able to discuss face-to-face the customer care offered by your company, encouraging them to offer their ideas and their views.

These can be very meaningful, especially if all departments of your company are represented.

4.3.6 Alternative solutions are presented positively to the customer

It is crucial, however, that action is taken on comments made by customers, as they soon get fed up with filling in questionnaires if no action is taken. So it is very important that the customer gets feedback of action taken by your company. Even if resources do not allow you to do what your customers would like, they know that you have listened.

4.3.7 Accurate advice is given to customers of relevant alternative sources of assistance outside the organisation

Handling customer complaints or problems is a skill that needs to be developed by all customer-facing personnel. However, whether you are dealing with customers face-to-face, on the telephone or by letter or questionnaire, you must always tell the truth. Passing the buck or telling white lies will never solve the problem - especially if the end result is that you need to go to arbitration by recommending the customer to the OFT or Society of Motor Manufacturers and Traders (SMMT).

LEVEL 3 - UNIT 5

INITIATE AND EVALUATE CHANGE TO IMPROVE SERVICE TO CUSTOMERS

5.1 Obtain and analyse feedback from customers

There are four elements to unit five. The first is:

5.1.1 Comments on organisational service are consistently sought from customers

It is important that, by sensitive questioning, you obtain meaningful information from your customers, about their experience of such things as:

- Being made to feel welcome.
- Getting an appointment within a reasonable period.
- Prompt attention when you arrived with your vehicle.
- Advice about the work needing to be done.
- The attention paid to any minor details you had reported.
- The work completed when promised.
- The quality of work carried out.
- The cleanliness of the vehicle when returned.
- The helpfulness and politeness of staff.
- The explanation of the invoice.
- The cost representing value for money.
- The availability of any parts required.

The above topics represent the majority of customer dissatisfaction problems.

5.1.2 Complaints and commendations from customers are used to analyse and evaluate relevant product or services

When seeking comments on your customer care it is important to ensure that you question as many of your customers as you can, as invariably those customers who were dissatisfied with your service are more likely to comment than those who were satisfied.

The key is to split your customers up into four categories: Completely Satisfied, Mostly Satisfied, Dissatisfied and Completely Dissatisfied.

The most worrying thing you will find is that as much as 10% of your customers will fall into the last category, yet very few of them would have passed comment to you had you not asked for their opinion.

5.1.3 New opportunities are generated to gain customer feedback

Other than the focus groups already mentioned in previous performance criteria, some retailers are carrying out exit polls. Talking to customers who are picking up their vehicles in the car park can give you an instant response as to how they feel they have been treated.

I conducted one of these exit polls and it was very surprising the comments given on our service. For example, most would have liked the reception team to have explained more fully the work which had been carried out for their bill of £156. Instead they were told how much it was, in a very pleasant manner. All courtesies were shown but, bearing in mind that when they get in the car they very often cannot see or feel any difference or benefit for the £156 just paid, they were left uncertain that any work had been done.

This exit poll did give me an opportunity to clarify any uncertainties the customer may have had.

From this exit poll I was able to introduce a simple service check sheet signed off by the technician (most companies have them, but we did not use them).

5.1.4 Customer feedback is analysed for patterns and themes and results are recorded and understood by others

Testimonials or commendations are just as important as complaints, as valuable feedback to what you and your company are doing correctly which motivated the customer to give you a pat on the back.

Used correctly, as well as motivating your team to try harder you can assess what gave customer delight and try to develop that part further.

5.1.5 Customer feedback is stored in the most appropriate place

Without doubt you will be the first to know if your company has had a bad CSS or CSI, as it will have been drawn to the attention of those at the highest level within your company by your supplier.

The skill is not to become paranoid about it. Use the reports constructively; remember the customer is using this questionnaire to tell you something. Customers who have not had a good experience will ALWAYS fill it in; those who have an average experience will NOT always fill it in; those who have had their expectations of their needs exceeded WILL fill it in.

Again it is worth looking at your strengths as well as your weaknesses so that you can identify what you and your company are doing correctly. Have another look at the sample analysis of the Rate-Our-Service cards in Level 2's Performance Criteria 3.1.4.

Customer feedback, if identifiable to a customer, should be recorded in either the customer history file or the vehicle file. A separate file should be kept to enable you to monitor complaints and problems to see if they are recurring on a regular basis. These should be discussed at least once a month at a quality or innovation meeting.

As I have said in previous performance criteria, customers get inundated with questionnaires and, unless we acknowledge their replies showing what action has been taken following their feedback, they stop giving their time to respond to your requests.

It is important that customers' comments are kept confidential and are not left about for non-company members to see. However, all testimonials and commendations should be displayed in the reception area for future clients to read. It is also important that all the company's employees see the letters, be they good or bad, as this can focus their attentions on the importance of customer care.

5.2 Proposed improvements in service delivery based on customer feedback

5.2.1 Proposed improvements to customer service are clearly presented in the appropriate form and are based on accurate information

As mentioned in previous performance criteria the suppliers' CSS or CSI are very detailed. Giving you performance percentages enables everyone clearly to understand the challenge. However, it is worth remembering the point made earlier: that only customers who have had a below-average service will be almost certain to complete the questionnaires. It is important that you carry out your own rate-our-service survey to ensure that the feedback you are getting is accurate.

5.2.2 Predictions are made about customer requirements and are based on the accurate interpretation of customer feedback

Together with your own records of customer feedback you should look towards the trends or patterns in both your strengths and weaknesses. For example, customer care could fall down dramatically during staff holidays, or when key personnel are on sick leave, and you can get a poor result especially at the time of registration changes or the start of a new year, when the volume of business is three times as much as normal. Again I would draw your attention to the text and the illustrations concerning the Rate-Our-Service initiatives in Level 2's Performance Criteria 3.1.4.

5.2.3 Concise information which accurately summarises proposed improvements is passed to appropriately targeted individuals

When action needs to be taken which is beyond your authority, it is important that you discuss it and consult with your close colleagues. By using all your team's brains, you can review the patterns and develop a strategy which can be documented and presented to your managers in a meaningful way. Using the data, with quantitive and qualitative evaluation methods, you can illustrate the benefits both to the company and to customer care.

5.3 Initiate changes in response to customer requirements

5.3.1 *Action is taken, within own area of authority, to remedy shortfalls in customer care*

One of the major problems in companies today is wasted time - for example, time taken by the customer to park their car, time taken by the receptionist to find the car to get the chassis details, time taken for the mechanic to find the car to start work on it and time taken for the customer to find their car again when they come to collect it.

How would you find an economical way of solving this problem, since it effects both your company and customer care operations?

Using the performance criteria of 5.4.3:

What is the problem? *Wasted time looking for the customer's car*
What is causing the problem? *No procedure for identifying location of the car each time it moves.*
What are the possible solutions? *Number the car park bays; buy roof numbers; or attach a label with map of the car park to the keys.*

5.3.2 *Action is taken to alert others to changes needed to improve customer service*

By discussing the problem of locating customers' cars with the reception team, with workshop control, with the technicians, and of course with the customer, you are able to produce ideas and possible changes to working practices and procedures which will improve customer care, with the full support and co-operation of the whole team. It is important that you document and communicate your findings to everyone who has taken part in solving the problem.

5.3.3 *Own initiatives are introduced which respond to customer requirements and are within own area of authority*

Let us assume that the general opinion was that attaching a label to the keys with a small map of the car park was thought to be the most effective solution of those suggested in 5.3.1 above.

The benefits would be that when the customer came into reception they indicated on the map where they had parked their car, with a line in the bay. This would enable the receptionist and the technician to find the vehicle straight away. When the technician had completed the work and parked the vehicle back in the car park they crossed off the first line and entered a new line on the map. This enables the receptionist to direct the customer immediately to where their vehicle is on collection.

The time saved each day in looking for cars will create additional hours to sell, and customers will not be wandering about in the dark looking for their vehicle. The same goes for movement of internal vehicles such as used cars or new vehicles in for Pre-Delivery Inspection (PDI).

5.3.4 Actions and initiatives are based on thorough analysis of appropriate data and take account of any predicted customer needs

So the key is to collect all the facts, exchange ideas and seek advice, consult with all the team concerned, ask the customers what they want, take account of possible needs of customers such as early-morning drop-off or late-night collection, then present a clear logical argument which addresses the solution to the problem.

5.3.5 Own ideas and experience are used to implement changes introduced by others

If the opinion of the team was that the car park should be numbered, or that roof numbers would be a better idea, it may be that this would be outside your area of authority.

Again, I can only stress that your skill in presenting the facts to your managers detailing the benefits to your company, the improved customer care and, of course, the relevant costs to implement the new changes, will need to be very professional to overcome any objections. Finally, offer to implement and pilot the new changes in procedures. This way you own the problem.

5.4 Evaluate changes designed to improve service to customers

5.4.1 Outcomes of changes to improve customer service are systematically monitored using all available feedback

Of course, the one way you can monitor changes and improvements is from the CSS or CSI reports that come in, either every month or quarter. However, as outlined previously, your own research by telephone follow-ups or by rate-our-service cards has to be the most important guide, as you are hearing first-hand from your customer.

You could also circulate a questionnaire around your own company, asking all the employees what they think about your customer-care procedures.

5.4.2 Implications of changes to products or services are identified and appropriate colleague(s) are informed

Having received input from your customers and colleagues and drawn up actions to rectify the shortfalls, it is of the utmost importance that all employees of your company are informed of the changes that are being implemented within your customer care procedures, giving the cause of the problem and the possible solution to the problem that you are to pilot.

This way all employees will understand and own the problem of ensuring that the solution works.

However, to establish and identify changes needed to improve customer care we need to develop the skill of BRAIN STORMING in groups and presenting the changes needed to your colleagues.

The key is to prepare a SUMMARY:

THE PROBLEM
- State it as a fact
- Limit it
- Clarify the terms of the problem
- Give some background

CAUSES
- Accept as many as possible
- Do not evaluate the cause immediately
- Summarize often

POSSIBLE SOLUTIONS
- Be specific
- Give evidence such as:
  - Statistics
  - Demonstration
  - Testimony
  - Incident
  - Exhibit
- Summarize often

THE BEST SOLUTION
- Review solutions and evidence
- Vote
- Agree action to be taken.

5.4.3   Recommendations on the effectiveness of changes designed to improve customer service are communicated to the appropriate colleague(s)

One of the hardest things to overcome in today's business world is the apathy shown by managers towards their teams.

The old saying 'When I want your opinion, I will give it to you' still is, regrettably, widespread.

Your skill is to overcome this apathy by careful presentation of the facts, showing what the problem is, what is causing the problem and what the possible solutions are, and presenting the best solution in report form, showing the change in procedures, how it will affect and benefit our customer care, and indicating the costs.

It is imperative that, for your own well-being and personal development, you develop the skill of problem solving, coming up with new ideas, being innovative, using the brains of all those around you and presenting the solutions in a way that your managers would be idiots not to heed.

I have here used an example of how I problem-solved with my teams, and produced the summary form overleaf so that it was easily understood, and showed my recommendations to improve customer care.

SUMMARY

WHAT IS THE PROBLEM ?
  TIME WASTED LOOKING FOR CUSTOMERS' CARS BY RECEPTION TEAM, MECHANICS, SALESMEN AND THE CUSTOMER.

WHAT IS CAUSING THE PROBLEM?
  NO PROCEDURE FOR IDENTIFYING LOCATION OF THE VEHICLE EACH TIME IT MOVES.

WHAT ARE POSSIBLE SOLUTIONS TO THE PROBLEM?
  NUMBER THE CAR PARKING BAYS, BUY ROOF MAGNETIC NUMBERS, ATTACH A LABEL WITH MAP OF CAR PARK TO THE KEYS.

WHAT IS THE BEST SOLUTION?
  PRODUCE AN INEXPENSIVE LABEL WITH MAP SO THAT VEHICLE CAN BE IDENTIFIED ON IT.

CONSIDER THIS . . .

WHY ARE WE IN BUSINESS? WHAT ARE OUR OBJECTIVES?

- To increase the profits of the company each year in order to achieve an acceptable or fair return on investment.
- To make more efficient use of all the resources used by the company, whether stock, storage space, sales areas or cash in circulation.
- To increase the profitability to allow future reinvestment which will permit the company to grow.
- To seek ways and means of making the company grow to provide improved working conditions, increased job satisfaction and future opportunities.
- To provide, at all times, the highest quality of customer service, ensuring that value for money is provided with courtesy and consideration.
- To portray an efficient, businesslike and professional image, at the same time as providing a highly personalised service.
- To accept criticism from customers as a basis for improving the level of service to all customers.
- To examine the organisation, system and methods used within the company with a view to improving customer service.
- To develop a company image that makes customers want to buy from us on the basis that 'We are easy to do business with'.
- To train and re-train all employees to keep them up-to-date with product knowledge, customer relations and selling skills through NVQs.
- By training to develop a team capable of running the operation using each others' brains for the well-being of the company.

INNOVATION - YOUR MOVE

Many articles, books and reports have been written about innovation in business but they have tended to concentrate on the manufacturing sector; too little attention has been paid to service and retailing.

What is innovation? It is the process of taking new ideas effectively and profitably to satisfy customers; it is a process of continual improvement involving the whole company and is an essential part of business strategy and everyday practice.

Why innovate? You are faced with intensifying competitive pressure. Demands from manufacturers, the motoring public, legislation, shareholders and even your colleagues with whom you work mean that to be achievers you must meet those challenges by providing a constant stream of new and improved processes and services.

What inhibits innovation? I know that in many companies the owners or senior executives believe that they alone know everything. 'When I want your opinion I will give it to you'.

So carved-in-stone attitudes and policies stay in place and the employees leave their brains at home.

Without doubt, this is the major cause of apathy towards being innovative and can stifle your entrepreneurial thinking. (**PLEASE, PLEASE do not allow this to happen to you. Our industry's future depends on people like you who are prepared to develop themselves by being qualified and being the best in your field of expertise**).

When senior executives do finally see the light, it is hard sometimes to get employees to react in a positive manner. Some say 'I am not paid to think', or they believe there is a catch because, as employees, they have never been asked for their opinion and in most cases never been listened to.

All the successful companies I have been involved with who are making good profits with the employees in secure employment had the same things in common.

- The company's leadership was the driving force.
- It demonstrated a clear sense of mission and purpose which was thoroughly thought out at board level, then communicated throughout the dealership to all the teams.
- The management was prepared to listen and actively used the brains of all the employees to the benefit of the company.
- The boss encouraged and managed risk-taking and change. He set challenging but realistic targets, although they might initially appear over-demanding.
- He communicated with customers, suppliers, investors and, most importantly, with you the employee.
- As a best-practice company he ensured an open, cross-functional and multi-level team approach to projects, engaged in problem solving and gave employees responsibility right down to the most junior level.

If your boss starts to ask for your opinion, give him every support and encouragement.

THE PATH TO INNOVATION

You do not need to wait for your bosses to become innovative, especially if you are looking for promotion and wanting to better yourself. Bearing in mind that you are studying for a National Vocational Qualification, you must have confidence in yourself to do it.

It will be important that you get the support of your immediate manager, use the NVQ portfolio as your reason for doing it and get him involved in helping you to arrange things.

There are six steps you can take:

- Step one: **form an assessment team.**

    By including people from all departments you are more likely to be able to analyse current practices, to get a true picture of problems which are affecting the bottom line and to take and be responsible for subsequent action. The team should be charged with assessing your company's current practices and performance, identifying gaps between current performance and best practice, such as by using composites, registration penetration reports etc, then developing and implementing action plans and setting perform-ance targets.

- Step two: **carry out an initial assessment.**

    The team should conduct an initial assessment of the employees' opinions as to what they believe are the strengths and weaknesses of the company. This can be done by sending out a simple questionnaire, asking everyone what they think the problems are and what causes them.

- Step three: **Choice of areas to focus on.**

    Following the initial assessment, you will have lots of areas of concern. First, eliminate the moans and groans - many of these cost very little to put right and if the rest of the company's employees see the innovation team caring about their concerns they will respond better to the company's concerns.

    Ask your boss what problems, if solved, would have a major impact on the bottom line (and I do not mean 'Sack the government' or 'Get our manufacturers to reduce our targets'). An example could be increasing showroom traffic, or reducing time spent waiting at the back counter, or improving the hourly recover rate, or increasing parts sales retail. These areas your innovation team can handle by using a technique such as that illustrated by the form shown at the end of the last chapter.

- Step four: **review in depth.**

  Each area identified as important by your team should now be reviewed in depth. Current practice and performance should be identified and documented to ensure maximum benefit. The review should be grounded in reality and honesty to reflect current practices, rather than just contain statements of policy. For example analysing the regs pen, examining the problem of slow-moving stock, looking at improvement of follow-up systems for all departments and examining credit control will all create stimulating discussion and give a much more realistic picture of performance.

  The result of this should be a better understanding of the firm's performance by non-managerial staff and provide accurate identification of the gaps to be closed. Are we doing what is required to match best practice companies?

- Step five: **Bench marking.**

  This step must be used if you are to keep ahead in your own market place and it must be reviewed carefully.

  Just as dealerships are 'mystery-shopped' by suppliers of vehicles, so you and your team need to carry out a similar procedure among your competitors.

  For example, using a telephone recorder, mystery-shop all garages within five miles of your company to establish how good their image really is on marketing, prices and customer telephone care. I think you may get a shock. These recordings played back to your own teams will allow them to bench-mark how good or bad they really are.

- Step six: **Closing the gaps.**

  Having identified gaps and their causes through self-assessment and bench-marking, the prime task is to take action to close them.

  The only way this can be done is through internal group brainstorming where the findings are presented and reviewed by the assessment team and other interested parties. Hopefully these will include your boss who, if he uses his brains, will respond in a positive manner, and allow you and your team to action your plans.

FOR YOUR FURTHER CONSIDERATION...

INNOVATION APPLIED IN A SERVICE DEPARTMENT

- using customer care performance criteria

So many of the principles which we have discussed in this book can be profitably applied to all departments, and indeed all businesses. For example, the following report outlines how an innovation team, over a two-day period, observed its workshop of 12 technicians and recorded all the time that could not be charged to the customer - that is, all the non-productive time.

This included such things as collecting protective covers for seats, finding technical information, walking time, finding special tools and equipment, waiting for parts, incorrect information on job cards, hours lost through waiting for authorization from fleet customers, waiting for job cards, looking for keys and so on.

At this dealership the innovation team - made up of people from sales, service, admin and parts - assessed that up to 7,130 hours out of a potential available to sell of 19,282 were lost in a year in non-productive wasted time.

The team set out to reduce this waste by 50%, knowing that the potential gross profit would be £114,636 from service and parts department if they could achieve it. This is the story of our endeavours.

The brief: **to identify wasted hours and decide what action could be taken to eliminate the waste.**

We started by looking at our own statistics and going back to basics.

Labour hours available = number of productive people, multiplied by the number of working days, multiplied by the number of hours per day.

This amounted to: 12 x 206 x 7.8 hours = 19,282 productive hours per year.

Average hourly recovery rate = £35 per hour

Total revenue potential = £674,870

Gross profit before direct expenses at 78%
(assuming everyone is 100% efficient) = £526,398

Using our innovation team, drawn from all departments, we obtained the cooperation of the productive staff to collate the non-productive time and identify the areas that needed to be tackled.

Over a two-day period, we established that, on an average day, each technician had to make up just over 2.88 hours to be 100% efficient, to compensate for the wasted time that was involved in doing his job.

This, estimated over 206 working days, came to 7,130 hours.

Observing activities over the course of two days, the team produced a list of the areas and times involved which required action if those hours were to be turned into productive hours.

Lost time per technician per day, mulitiplied by the 12 technicians and the 206 days gave these figures.

Computer down time	not observed
Obstructions in the workshop	not observed
Finding technical information	124 hours
Cleaning time	41 hours
Walking time	1,242 hours
Protective covers in cars	82 hours
Clocking on and off jobs	246 hours
Waiting for authorization	371 hours
Emptying oil drainers	41 hours
Wrong parts supplied	82 hours
Parking and collecting cars	288 hours
Incorrect/insufficient infoon the job card	164 hours
Looking for special equipment	412 hours
Looking for special tools	82 hours
Waiting for parts/back counter	2,060 hours
Completing check sheets/paperwork	412 hours
Looking for cars in car park	618 hours
Looking for keys	412 hours
Waiting for job cards	453 hours
Total hours in a year	7,130 hours

(and some of these times were conservative).

At £35 per hour, 7,130 hours represented £249,550 lost sales. So out of a potential sales of £674,870 we were wasting £249,550, some 37% of our potential sales. At 75% gross profit that came to £187,162.

So how did our team overcome losing this important income and gross profit potential? We did it by using our innovation team's brains and ideas.

Our team were encouraged to 'brain storm' carefully the areas that needed to be looked at, to go out and look at best-practice bench marking - that is, going to other dealerships who were doing it right. Then, by assessing the composites available to us through Alison Associates, and by seeking the input from our own teams, we should be able to reduce the waste by at least 50%.

The following text shows how we tackled the problems and some of the solutions the team came up with.

When you see them you will understand what I mean by looking at carved-in-stone policies in an innovational way, because most of them do not cost a lot to implement and could be well within your own and your team's responsibility. These are the things that were decided:

FINDING TECHNICAL INFORMATION
124 HOURS LOST SALES = £4,340.
Relocate the microfiche reader near workshop control.
Relocate workshop bulletins near workshop control.
Master technician to be responsible for updates.
Daily check to be made to see that all microfiche files were available.

CLEANING TIME
41 HOURS LOST SALES = £1,435
General overhaul of procedures organised.

WALKING TIME
1242 HOURS LOST SALES = £43,470
Move workshop control near parts back-counter.
Key tag to show location of cars.
Protective covers to be fitted by apprectices.
Supply watering cans for each technician.
Provide oil and water drainers - one between two technicians.
Put air pressure gauges in one place.
Move clocking machine near workshop control.
Supply paper towel rolls, one per bay.
Keep special tools and equipment in one place.
All technicians to have tags to exchange for special tools.

PROTECTIVE COVER IN CARS
82 HOURS LOST SALES = £2,870

Apprentice or retired person to fit when collecting mileage's and chassis rubbings (see suggestion under 'Walking Time').

CLOCKING ON AND OFF JOBS
246 HOURS LOST SALES = £8,610

Workshop controller to clock all jobs on and off.

Move clocking machine near to workshop control.

Working hours staggered to smooth bottlenecks.

Consider technicians should not clock in or out each day. Trust?

WAITING FOR AUTHORIZATION
371 HOURS LOST SALES £12,985

Technicians to investigate add-on work first, before carrying out service, so that service can be done while waiting for authority.

Stagger working hours to smooth out authorization requests by reception.

Service manager to assist in obtaining authorizations between 10am and 11am.

Consider using the fax to obtain authority, order numbers etc.

Consider telephoning the day before when you know order numbers are required.

Try to get retail customers to authorize in advance a limit in £s for additional work, such as £30, £40 or £50.

Consider quoting 15% in excess of the cost, then reduce it when customers come in to pay (customer delight) but would allow cover for wiper blades, bulbs etc.

EMPTYING OIL DRAINERS
41 HOURS LOST SALES = £1,435

General overhaul of procedures organised.

WRONG PARTS SUPPLIED
82 HOURS LOST SALES £2,870

Receptionist, retiree or apprentice must ensure full information is on the job card, including engine number and prefix etc.

Ensure back-counter parts persons are well trained and understand the use of EPC and microfiche.

PARKING THE FINISHED JOB (Finding Space)
288 HOURS LOST SALES = £10,080

Parking location to be marked on a new-design key tag.

Consider issuing bleepers to customers without phone contact to collect early.

Consider delivery and collection, using retired drivers, as a properly organised operation, not just as and when.

Extend hours of operation; organise overnight loan cars and service between 6 and 8pm - customer collects car at 8am and returns loan car.

INSUFFICIENT/INCORRECT INFORMATION ON JOB CARDS
164 HOURS LOST SALES = £5,740

Receptionist to obtain full and accurate information when customer books in for service over telephone, and to specify the problems correctly.

Check-sheet to be prepared to assist receptionists/telephonists to ask the correct questions.

Receptionists must be identified on the job card for technicians to refer to.

Workshop controller to check job cards night before to ensure sufficient information is provided.

Attach service history from the computer if available on to the job card.

LOOKING FOR SPECIAL EQUIPMENT
412 HOURS LOST SALES = £14,420

Establish list of required equipment.

Carry out inventory and replace missing or broken equipment.

Check number of watering cans.

Check number of pressure bleeders.

Check number of coolant drain trays.

Check number of oil drainers - at least one per oil dispenser.

Check number of paper towel rolls, investigate costs, have them strategically placed.

Have specific location for air pressure gauges and watering cans.

LOOKING FOR SPECIAL TOOLS
82 HOURS LOST SALES = £2,870

Take inventory of special tools.

Replace missing or broken tools where required.

Control movement of tools by tag system.

Tool boards to be checked each night.

Register required so that missing tools or broken tools can be ordered.

WAITING FOR PARTS/BACK COUNTER

2060 HOURS LOST SALES = £72,100

Stagger working hours of the techs to smooth demands on back counter.

Ensure back counter is operational through lunch hours.

Investigate parts department making up service kits in advance for jobs already booked in the night before, ie pre-picking.

Parts and reception to communicate more in relation to non-stock item job coming in.

COMPLETING ISO 9002 CHECK SHEETS

412 HOURS LOST = £14,420

Consider training apprentice or retiree to complete check sheet when taking chassis rubbings, mileages and fitting seat covers.

LOOKING FOR CAR IN PARK

618 HOURS LOST SALES = £21,630

Improve signing in customer park.

Number parking bays.

Bay numbers to be entered on key tags by apprentice retiree or receptionist.

Place signs in the car park requesting customers to bring in service books plus location of parked car.

Tester to amend the bay number to enable reception to notify customer on collection.

Produce tag with outline of the car park so the location can be marked on it, and so technicians will also find it quickly.

LOOKING FOR KEYS

412 HOURS LOST SALES = £14,420

Customers' keys to be tagged immediately and located on key board, for WIP vehicles only; separate board to be used for sales, loan cars and VOR.

WAITING FOR JOB CARDS

453 HOURS LOST SALES = £15,855

Set up job-card rack for each technician.

Workshop controller to put next job into each rack, so as to be ready for
first thing each day.

Consider having a salesman per week to assist reception between 7.30
and 9.30am.

Consider employing a retired person to handle seat covers, take mileages,
chassis rubbings and parking locations (as suggested under other
heading).

Reception to consider encouraging customers to bring vehicles in earlier
in mornings.

If previous suggestion is successful, reception to start at 7am and second
person at 7.30am.

Staggered working hours for technicians to be more evenly spread, 50%
at 8am and 50% at 8.30am.

Courtesy driver to start at 7am to ferry customers as required.

Apprentice to start at 7am to obtain mileages and chassis rubbings etc.

So there we have it, lost hours of 7,130. If, by putting in most of the
suggestions put up by the innovation team we reduce the lost hours by
50%, our potential increase in service turnover would be £124,775.

You might be able to use some ideas from this report in your own
company.

GLOSSARY

Back Order	Parts that the factory are temporarily out of stock.
C.S.I	Customer Satisfaction Indicators
C.S.S	Customer Satisfaction Surveys.
I.F.C	Inter Firm Comparisons.
M.O.T	Ministry Of Transport Test
O.F.T	Office of Fair Trading.
P.D.I	Pre-Delivery Inspection.
Retailers	Dealerships or Independent Garages.
R.O.S	Rate our service.
S.M.M.T	Society of Motor Manufacturers and Traders.
Suppliers	Manufacturers or Importers.
T.E.Cs	Training and Enterprise Councils
T.P order	Top Priority parts order.
Units	Vehicles.
Vin Number	Part or body identification number.
V.O.R	Vehicle off the road.
W.I.P	Work in progress.

Index: Customer Service

A

authority
financial 72-3
operational 73
personal 36, 48
personnel 73

B

BM90 43, 53
body language 26-7
brain storming 90-1
business, reasons for/objectives
concerning 93

C

colleagues
alerting to changes in procedures
43
alerting to potential shortfalls 36-7
concise, accurate information
passed to 87
giving/offering help to 5, 8-9, 30,
39, 48-9, 62
informed of improvements within
own area of responsibility 42
informed of recurring
problems/complaints 81-2

informed of
implications/effectiveness of
changes/solutions to problems
82, 90-1
organisational procedures
evaluated with 42-3
potential new procedures
identified, explored and agreed
with 80
and problem solving 31, 33, 59
and service reliability 40-1, 43
sharing of ideas, knowledge and
experience 8, 42
updating of product/service
knowledge 6
working relationship with 6-9

communication
difficulties acknowledged and help
sought 30
with relevant outside parties 51-2
suited to customer needs 29-30,
83
telephone 57
understanding of checked 30
written and spoken language 29
see also customer communication

complaints
customer procedures 27-8, 79-80

own ideas/experience used to
    implement changes introduced
    by others 89
own initiatives introduced 88-9
proposed improvements presented
    in appropriate form based on
    accurate information 87

customers
additional suggestions for 2
avoidance of friction with 75-6
balancing needs of organisation
    with 24, 72-5
feedback from 40-1, 85-6
feelings acknowledged and
    behaviour adapted accordingly
    26
feelings judged accurately 26
feelings regularly checked 26-7, 68
improving working relationship
    21-2
making them feel welcome 8
minimising conflict with
    organisation 24-5
needs explored and met 3, 38-9,
    64, 68, 72
organising work patterns to needs
    of 48-50
presentation of personal image to
    69-71
proposals put to clearly recorded
    and stored 25
protected from unnecessary worry
    4-5, 56-7
reasons for failures explained 4
relevant procedures for complaints
    27-8
security of information on 18-19
solving problems for 31-7
storage of information on 10-14,
    25
suggestions for improvements in
    records 46

E

equipment and supplies, as available,
    up-to-date and in good order 70

F

feedback
analysed, recorded and understood
    85
colleagues informed of service
    reliability improvements 40-1
comments on service consistently
    sought 40
existing procedures actively used
    and outcomes regularly
    reported 40
improvements to service reliability
    initiated 40
new opportunities generated to
    gain 85
predictions made based on 87
stored in appropriate place 85-6
finance 72-3

I

information
disclosure of confidential items
    18-19
given to customers 4-5
improving system of 13
maintainance and location 10-11
monitoring and recording 11-12,
    25
options/alternatives identified and
    offered 15
out-of-date 12
overdue 12
routine scanning of 52
sharing 43
sources correctly identified and
    accessed 15

supplied in appropriate form 17-18

supplied within required deadlines 18

systems for return implemented 12

transcribing and compiling 17

understanding requirements 15

work practice conforms to organisational requirements 13-14

innovation

case history 97-103

defined 93-4

inhibitions to 94

reasons for 94

six steps towards 95-6

in successful companies 94-5

Inter Firm Comparisons (IFC) 43, 53

Investment in People programmes 53

M

MIDAS 43, 53

Mobility Schemes 62

O

Office of Fair Trading (OFT) 33, 36, 79-80

organisation

balancing needs of customer 24, 72-5

limitations clearly and positively explained 24, 74

minimising conflict with customer 24-5

options for mutual gain as cost effective 73-4

options for mutual gains identified and relevant parties informed 73

recognition of limitations and seeking assistance 25

P

personal image

appearance and behaviour 70

availability of equipment and supplies 70

courteous and helpful 69-70

group responsibility 21

organizational standards for 20-1

own behaviour consistently conveys positive image of organisation 71

positive 20

resilience and adapting to stress 23, 69

working relationship with customers 21-2, 70-1

personnel 73

problem solving

action taken within own area of authority 36

alerting colleagues to potential shortfalls 36-7

alternative products or services 33

on behalf of customers 77-83

clearly summarised 31

in co-operation with others 36

colleagues consulted 31, 33, 59

customers' perceptions identified and acknowledged 31, 77

organisational 33

recurring complaints 32

service delivery checked 35-6

standard procedures activated 35

understanding proposals and reasons for them 34

see also complaints; customer problems

product delivery

action taken to prevent shortfalls 36

additional 2

alerting colleagues to potential shortfalls 36-7

checked and problems passed to appropriate authority 35-6

continual updating of own knowledge 3

customers informed promptly 56

needs explored 3

prompt supply 2

as solutions to problems 33

R

Rate-Our-Service questionnaires 22, 43, 47, 52, 86

records

clearly stored and relayed 75

conform to relevant statutory obligations and requirements 47

documentation as comprehensive, correct and relevant 45

facts set out clearly and concisely 45

for monitoring service delivery 47

regularly and accurately checked and up-dated 46

suggestions for improvement clearly based on customer needs 46

suggestions for improvement suitably delivered to appropriate authority 46-7

S

security

customer information 18-19

records conform to relevant statutory obligations and requirements 47

service delivery

action taken to prevent shortfalls in 36

active use of collaborative work with others 53

additional 2

alerting colleagues to potential shortfalls 36-7

checked and problems passed to appropriate authority 35-6

continual updating of own knowledge 3

customers informed promptly 56

customers kept updated about interruptions 4

evaluate changes for improvement 90-2

information given to customers designed to protect them from unnecessary worry 4-5

initiate changes in response to customer requirements 88-9

maintaining 4-6

needs explored 3

obtain/analyse feedback from customers 84-6

practical help offered to colleagues 5

prompt supply 2

proposed improvements based on customer feedback 87

reasons for failures 4

sharing of knowledge and experience 8

as solutions to problems 33

use of records 47

service reliability

current procedures used flexibly 38-9